PROGRESS IN EDUCATION

OVERCOMING FOREIGN LANGUAGE CLASSROOM ANXIETY

PROGRESS IN EDUCATION

Additional books in this series can be found on Nova's website
under the Series tab.

Additional E-books in this series can be found on Nova's website
under the E-book tab.

EDUCATION IN A COMPETITIVE AND GLOBALIZING WORLD

Additional books in this series can be found on Nova's website
under the Series tab.

Additional E-books in this series can be found on Nova's website
under the E-book tab.

PROGRESS IN EDUCATION

OVERCOMING FOREIGN LANGUAGE CLASSROOM ANXIETY

JINYAN HUANG

Nova Science Publishers, Inc.
New York

For permission to use material from this book please contact us:
Telephone 631-231-7269; Fax 631-231-8175
Web Site: http://www.novapublishers.com

NOTICE TO THE READER

Library of Congress Cataloging-in-Publication Data

Huang, Jinyan.
Overcoming anxiety in foreign language classrooms / Jinyan Huang.
p. cm.
Includes bibliographical references and index.
ISBN 978-1-61324-775-4 (alk. paper)
1. Language and languages--Study and teaching--Psychological aspects. 2. Anxiety. 3. Language and emotions. I. Title.
P53.7.H725 2011
418.0071--dc23
2011016760

Published by Nova Science Publishers, Inc. †New York

DEDICATION

I dedicate this book to my dearest wife, Shuangli, and my lovely children Joy, Jerry, and Jayden.

CONTENTS

LIST OF TABLES

PREFACE

Anxiety is an area that has received much attention in educational research in the past few decades (Abu-Rabia, 2004; Donley, 1999; Garcia, 1998; MacIntyre and Gardner, 1989; Spielberger, 1972, 1983; Young, 1990, 1991). It is defined as "the subjective feeling of tension, apprehension, nervousness, and worry associated with an arousal of the autonomic nervous system" (Spielberger, 1983, p. 1). It can refer to not only a person's stable personality but also his or her transitory emotional state.

Foreign language anxiety is widely used to describe the feeling of tension and apprehension, which is specifically associated with second language contexts, including speaking, listening, and learning (Dewaele, 2007). It is a distinct complex of self-perceptions, beliefs, feelings, and behaviors related to classroom language learning arising from the uniqueness of the language-learning process (Aida, 1994; MacIntyre and Gardner, 1991).

Related to *foreign language anxiety* is *language-skill-specific anxiety*, which refers to listening, speaking, reading, and writing anxiety in the learning of a foreign language. In general, students who struggle with anxiety are more likely to struggle with reading, writing, and most notably, listening comprehension and speaking (Cheng, Horwitz, and Shallert, 1999; Young, 1992). Research shows that students, regardless of anxiety within a specific category of *language-skill-specific anxiety*, tend to have a general feeling of low self-confidence (Cheng et al., 1999).

Related to *foreign language anxiety* and *language-skill-specific anxiety*, and fairly recently identified as distinguished from other forms of anxiety is *foreign language classroom anxiety* (FLCA) (von Wörde, 1998). FLCA is a more general type of anxiety in learning a foreign language with a strong speaking anxiety element and "low self-confidence" and is identified as an important component of FLCA construct (Cheng et al., 1999). Research also indicates that FLCA is a complex, multi-dimensional phenomenon (Young, 1992). There are many potential sources of learners' anxiety in the foreign language classrooms (Bailey, 1983; Garrett and Young, 2009; Horwitz, 2001; Horwitz and Young, 1991; Lucas, 1984; Yan and Horwitz, 2008). FLCA interferes with the acquisition, retention, and production of the new language (MacIntyre and Gardner, 1991; Saito and Samimy, 1996).

It is believed that FLCA has a debilitating effect on learners' learning of a foreign language, and both students and teachers should be responsible for reducing anxiety in foreign language classrooms (Abu-Rabia, 2004; Casado and Dereshiwsky, 2001; Chen and Chang, 2004; Donley, 1996; Ewald, 2007; Huang, Eslami, and Hu, 2010; Imai, 2010; Kim, 2009; Lucas, 1984; Naughton, 2006; Nakatani, 2010; Onwuegbuzie, Bailey, and Daley, 1997; Saito and Samimy, 1996; Semmar, 2010; Yan and Horwitz, 2008; Young, 1990, 1991; Zhao, 2007).

A large number of empirical studies on FLCA have been conducted in a variety of contexts in the world. For example, many studies were conducted in the contexts of learning Spanish, French, German, Japanese, Latin, and Russian as foreign languages and English as a second language in the United States (Allen and Herron, 2003; Casado and Dereshiwsky, 2001; Duxbury and Tsai, 2010; Ewald, 2007; Frantzen and Magnan, 2005; Ganschow and Sparks, 1996; Kitano, 2001; Marcos-Llinás and Garau, 2009; Onwuegbuzie et al., 1997; Saito and Samimy, 1996; Sellers, 2000; Sparks and Ganschow, 2007; Tallon , 2009; Tittle , 1997; von Wörde, 1998). Further, several studies were conducted in the context of learning English as a foreign language and learning other foreign languages in Taiwan (Chen and Chang, 2009; Chen and Chang, 2004; Cheng et al., 1999; Duxbury and Tsai, 2010; Huang et al., 2010; Wu, 2010), Qatar (Semmar, 2010); Korea (Kim, 2009), Iran (Noormohamadi, 2009), Hungary (Piniel, 2006), Israel (Abu-Rabia, 2004), Chile (Gregersen and Horwitz, 2002), and Venezuela (Rodriguez and Abreu, 2003). However, only a few studies were conducted in the context of learning English as a foreign language in China (Liu and Jackson, 2008; Yan and Horwitz, 2008; Zhao, 2007), further, no study examined FLCA-related issues in the context of learning other languages in China.

China, a country with the largest population in the world, has a very different educational system and cultural environment (Huang and Brown, 2009). Many foreign languages are being taught at all high schools and colleges and universities in China. English is a major foreign language that requires most students to learn. In addition, other Western languages such as

French, Spanish, and German, and several non-Western languages such as Japanese, Korean, and Arabic are all being taught at Chinese colleges and universities. In Chinese universities, students can choose to study a foreign language either as their major or non-major that meets the foreign language requirement by the Ministry of Education in China (Ministry of Education of China, 1999, 2003). Considering the large number of students learning foreign languages in Chinese universities and little research conducted in this area, it is of great importance to explore the factors contributing to Chinese university students' FLCA; the effects of gender, major, and language on their FLCA levels; and the ways to alleviate their FLCA levels. Accordingly, two empirical FLCA studies were conducted in the contexts of 855 Chinese freshmen university students learning different foreign languages at three major universities in Beijing, China.

These two studies attempt to a) examine the level of FLCA experienced by these 855 Chinese freshmen students, b) investigate the effects of gender (males vs. females), major (English majors vs. non-English majors), and language (English vs. other Western languages vs. non-Western languages) on the FLCA experienced by these Chinese freshmen students, c) uncover the causes of FLCA, and d) provide implications that help teachers and students connect their passion to teach and learn a foreign language in a stress-free classroom environment. This book, which is based on the two empirical studies, addresses FLCA issues in a variety of foreign language learning and teaching contexts from both theoretical and empirical perspectives. It contains nine chapters, and each chapter presents a main theme.

Chapter 1 explains and discusses what anxiety is in foreign language classrooms and how FLCA affects learners in learning a foreign language. It first defines key terms related to anxiety in foreign language classrooms. It then describes anxiety in language acquisition theories and teaching methods. Finally, it discusses the causes of anxiety, its impact on language learning, and how it can be reduced in foreign language classrooms.

Chapter 2 provides an overview of current research on FLCA by briefly reviewing 30 related studies that were conducted in the last 15 years (1996 ~ 2010). For many decades, anxiety has been studied by psychologists and educators from multiple perspectives, and its impact on cognitive, affective, and behavioural developments is well documented (MacIntyre and Gardner, 1991; von Wörde, 1998). However, only fairly recently has FLCA been identified as distinguished from other forms of anxiety (Foss and Reitzel, 1988; Horwitz, 1986; Horwitz, Horwitz, and Cope, 1986; Horwitz and Young, 1991; MacIntyre and Gardner, 1989, 1991; Price, 1991; von Wörde, 1998;

Young, 1990, 1991, 1992). Chapter 2 first identifies and describes these 30 studies on FLCA. It then reviews the research methods used in current FLCA research. Further, it categorizes the major topics investigated and summarizes the major findings of current FLCA research. Finally, this chapter identifies research gaps and discusses directions for future FLCA research.

Chapter 3 provides an overview of the two empirical studies included in this book. Considering the large number of students learning foreign languages in Chinese universities and little research conducted in this area, it is of great importance to explore the factors contributing to Chinese university students' FLCA; the effects of gender, major, and language on their FLCA levels; and the ways to reduce their FLCA levels. The chapter first discusses the rationale and context of these two empirical studies. It then describes their purposes, participants, and the instruments used for data collection. Finally, this chapter describes the data collection procedures, the data analysis methods, and how the results are reported.

Chapter 4 discusses the effect of gender on FLCA. Many studies have examined the impact of gender on learners' FLCA (Abu-Rabia, 2004; Clarck and Trafford, 1995; Dewaele, 2007; Ipek, 2009; Kitano, 2001; MacIntyre, Baker, Clément, and Donovan, 2002; Zhao, 2007). This chapter first briefly summarizes the previous literature regarding the gender effect on FLCA. As mentioned above, both empirical studies included in this book examined the gender effect on the FLCA experienced by the Chinese university freshmen students. This chapter then briefly describes the research methodology that both studies used to examine the gender effect. Further, it reports the gender-related results of both studies. Finally, this chapter discusses these results from the two studies.

Chapter 5 discusses the effect of major on FLCA. Whether or not learning a foreign language as a major can have an impact on the FLCA experienced by its learners (Chen and Chang, 2009; Cheng, Horwitz, and Schallert, 1999; Ewald, 2007; Liu and Jackson, 2008; Rodríguez and Abreu, 2003; Wu, 2010; Yan and Horwitz, 2008). For example, foreign language majors have more exposure to the language and are usually confident in their language skills; further, they spend much effort and time studying the language and tend to use a variety of foreign language-learning strategies more frequently. Therefore, they usually feel less anxious in the foreign language classroom than the non-major students (Wu, 2010). This chapter first briefly summarizes the previous literature regarding the effect of major on FLCA. As mentioned above, the first empirical study included in this book examined the effect of major on the FLCA experienced by the Chinese freshmen students at two major universities in Beijing. This chapter then briefly describes the research methodology that the first empirical study used to examine the major (English majors vs. non-English majors) effect. Further, it reports the major-related results of the study. Finally, this chapter discusses the results of the study.

Chapter 6 discusses the effect of language on FLCA. The specific foreign language that learners are learning can have an impact on their FLCA. For example, research shows that non-Western languages such as Japanese, Arabic, Chinese, and Korean are more difficult to learn than Western languages such as English and French, and therefore, can cause higher levels of anxiety (Aida, 1994). This chapter first briefly summarizes the previous literature regarding the effect of language on FLCA. As mentioned above, the second empirical study included in this book examined the effect of language on the FLCA experienced by the Chinese freshmen students at one major language university in Beijing. This chapter then briefly describes the research methodology that the second empirical study used to examine the language (English vs. other Western languages vs. non-Western languages) effect. Further, it reports the language-related results of the study. Finally, this chapter discusses the results of the study.

Chapter 7 discusses the sources of FLCA. Many studies have shown that foreign language classroom anxiety (FLCA) has multiple sources (Abu-Rabia, 2004; Allen and Herron, 2003; Casado and Dereshiwsky, 2001; Chen and Chang, 2004; Chen and Chang 2009; Ewald, 2007; Kim, 2009; Onwuegbuzie et al., 1997; Piniel, 2006; Saito and Samimy, 1996; Semmar, 2010; von Wörde, 1998; Wu, 2010; Yan and Horwitz, 2008; Young, 1990; Zhao, 2007). For example, von Wörde (1998) indicates that some sources may be associated with the student, the teacher, and the teaching methodology used by the teacher in language classrooms. Further, FLCA may also originate in "low self-esteem, specious beliefs regarding the learning of language, negative experience associated with the foreign language or culture, or the general experience of language learning" (p. 4). This chapter first briefly summarizes the previous literature regarding the sources of FLCA. As mentioned above, both empirical studies included in this book examined the sources of FLCA as reported by the Chinese university freshmen students. This chapter then briefly describes the research methodology that both studies used to examine the sources of FLCA. Further, it reports the research findings of both studies. Finally, this chapter discusses the similarities and differences in reporting sources of FLCA between the two empirical studies.

Chapter 8 discusses students' responsibilities for reducing their own FLCA. Students should take responsibility for their own foreign language learning (Rubin and Thompson, 1982). They have certain responsibilities for reducing their foreign language classroom anxiety (FLCA) (Cauce, Felner, and Primavera, 1982; Crookall and Oxford, 1991; Dewaele, Petrides, and Furnham, 2008; Donley, 1996; Foss and Reitzel, 1988; Hartup, 1989; Huang et al., 2010; Nakatani, 2010; Noormohamadi, 2009; Semmar, 2010; von Wörde, 1998; Wentzel, 1994; Young, 1991). For example, they should be aware of the types of anxiety they face in the foreign language classrooms and try to reduce their FLCA in order to manage and take control of their foreign language learning. Further, they should become familiar with their own language-learning styles and develop effective strategies to reduce their FLCA (Semmar, 2010). This chapter first briefly summarizes the previous literature. As mentioned above, both empirical studies included in this book examined students' responsibilities for reducing their own FLCA as reported by the Chinese university freshmen students. This chapter then briefly describes the research methodology that both studies used to examine students' responsibilities. Further, it reports the research findings of both studies. Finally, this chapter discusses the similarities and differences in reporting students' responsibilities for reducing FLCA between the two empirical studies.

Chapter 9 discusses foreign language teachers' responsibilities for reducing their students' FLCA. Research shows that teachers can create FLCA for their students, and therefore should be responsible for reducing their students' FLCA (Abu-Rabia, 2004; Casado and Dereshiwsky, 2001; Chen and Chang, 2004; Ewald, 2007; Kim, 2009; Lucas, 1984; Onwuegbuzie et al., 1997; Wu, 2010; Yan and Horwitz, 2008; Young, 1990; Zhao, 2007). This chapter first briefly summarizes the previous literature. As mentioned above, both empirical studies included in this book examined teachers' responsibilities for reducing their students' FLCA as reported by the Chinese university freshmen students. This chapter then briefly describes the research methodology that both studies used to examine teacher responsibilities for alleviating their students' FLCA. Further, it reports the research findings of both studies. Finally, this chapter discusses the similarities and differences in reporting teacher responsibilities for reducing their students' FLCA between the two empirical studies.

This book provides substantial and detailed information on the factors contributing to Chinese university students' FLCA; the effects of gender, major, and language on the FLCA experienced by Chinese university students; and the ways to alleviate their FLCA levels. This book provides important implications for foreign and second language students and teachers as well as expanding our understanding of FLCA issues in the context of learning and teaching both Western and non-Western languages.

ACKNOWLEDGMENTS

My thanks should first be expressed to my dearest wife Shuangli, my lovely daughter, Joy, and my two cute boys, Jerry and Jayden, who made great sacrifices in order for me to have time to work on this book. I, therefore, dedicate this book to my wife and three children.

I then would like to acknowledge my indebtedness and gratitude and register my sincere thanks to Dr. Yizhong Ning and Dr. Ping Wu, from Beijing Language and Culture University, Dr. Lisha Chen from Beijing Forestry University, and Professor Yeke Ru, from China University of Geosciences for their assistance with my data collection.

I also would like to thank Dr. Horwitz for granting me permission to use the Foreign Language Classroom Anxiety Scale (FLCAS) (Horwitz, Horwitz, and Cope, 1986) for my studies. In addition, I thank all the participants for their participation in my studies.

My final thanks should be expressed to Ms. Amanda Finn, my former research assistant from Niagara University, for her assistance with my data entry and initial analysis.

Chapter 1

ANXIETY IN FOREIGN LANGUAGE CLASSROOMS

ABSTRACT

Anxiety is a common phenomenon in people's learning processes. It prevents learners from completing academic tasks successfully, and so it interrupts academic learning (Garcia, 1998). Anxiety in foreign language-learning[1] classrooms leads to deficits in learning a foreign language (MacIntyre and Gardner, 1989). This chapter explains and discusses what anxiety is in foreign language classrooms and how it affects learners in learning a foreign language. It first defines key terms related to anxiety in foreign language classrooms. It then describes anxiety in language acquisition theories and teaching methods. Finally, it discusses the causes of anxiety, its impact on language learning, and how it can be reduced in foreign language classrooms.

KEY TERMS RELATED TO ANXIETY IN FOREIGN LANGUAGE CLASSROOMS

Anxiety is an area that has been received much attention in educational research in the past few decades (Abu-Rabia, 2004; Donley, 1999; Garcia, 1998; MacIntyre and Gardner, 1989; Spielberger, 1972, 1983; Young, 1990,

---

[1] Foreign language learning, second language learning and language learning, which are terms often used interchangeably in the literature, refer to the learning of "any language other than the first language" (Lightbown and Spada, 1993, p. 124).

1991). It is defined as "the subjective feeling of tension, apprehension, nervousness, and worry associated with an arousal of the autonomic nervous system" (Spielberger, 1983, p. 1). It can refer to not only a person's stable personality but also his or her transitory emotional state. Accordingly, two anxiety constructs have been developed: *state* anxiety and *trait* anxiety. A distinction between *state* and *trait* anxiety has become commonplace (Spielberger, 1972, 1983). *State anxiety* is defined as an unpleasant emotional arousal in face of threatening demands or dangers such as taking a test. A cognitive appraisal of threat is a prerequisite for the experience of this emotion (Spielberger, 1972). *Trait anxiety*, on the other hand, reflects the existence of stable individual differences in the tendency to respond with state anxiety in the anticipation of threatening situations (Lazarus, 1991).

In addition to *state* and *trait* anxiety, the term *situation-specific anxiety* has been used in the study of anxiety. According to MacIntyre and Gardner (1991), *foreign language anxiety*, language-skill-specific anxiety (e.g., listening anxiety, speaking anxiety, reading anxiety, and writing anxiety), test anxiety, and classroom anxiety belong to that category.

Foreign language anxiety is widely used to describe the feeling of tension and apprehension that is specifically associated with second language contexts, including speaking, listening, and learning (Dewaele, 2007). It is a distinct complex of self-perceptions, beliefs, feelings, and behaviors related to classroom language learning arising from the uniqueness of the language-learning process (Aida, 1994; Horwitz, Horwitz, and Cope, 1986; MacIntyre and Gardner, 1991). MacIntyre and Gardner (1991) argue that *foreign language anxiety* develops when the student feels under pressure or uncomfortable in a foreign language-learning situation. Therefore, it has a negative impact on the learning of a foreign language and must be responsible for students' uncomfortable experiences in foreign language classrooms (Horwitz, 2001; Horwitz et al., 1986; Rodriguez and Abreu, 2003).

Foreign language anxiety has the following three components: 1) communication apprehension, 2) test anxiety, and 3) fear of negative evaluation (Horwitz, 2001; Horwitz et al., 1986; Rodriguez and Abreu, 2003). Communication apprehension indicates a student's discomfort in talking in front of others. Although some students may be aware of their thoughts, their inability to express these thoughts in the foreign language or to understand what another person is saying can easily lead to hesitation and frustration. Further, test anxiety is common among students learning a foreign language. Some students may even view foreign language learning as a test situation, rather than an opportunity to communicate with others (Gregersen and

Horwitz, 2002). Finally, some students who fear negative evaluation are overly concerned with academic and personal evaluations of performance and competence in the foreign language. They often feel uncomfortable speaking in front of their peers because they lack the confidence and fear ridicule and awkwardness (Gregersen and Horwitz, 2002; Horwitz et al., 1986). All these three components of *foreign language anxiety* can have lasting and sometimes damaging effects on the progress of foreign language students (MacIntyre and Gardner, 1989). The essence of *foreign language anxiety* is the threat to an individual's self-concept, which is caused by the inherent limitations of communicating in an imperfectly mastered foreign language (Saito, Garaza, and Horwitz, 1999).

MacIntyre and Gardner (1989) further argue that *foreign language anxiety* occurs at the three stages of the second language acquisition (SLA) process, input, processing, and output. At the input stage, students experience anxiety when they're presented with new vocabulary, phrases, and sentences in the target language. Anxiety in the processing stage occurs when students try to organize and store input. During the output stage, anxiety occurs when students have to show their ability to recall previously learned materials (Onwuegbuzie, Bailey, and Daley, 2000). The impact of *foreign language anxiety* can be either facilitating or debilitating. When it facilitates learning, students' motivation can be increased, which leads to better performance (Ehrman and Oxford, 1995; Young, 1992). Debilitating anxiety impedes learning by causing students to have feelings of fear, doubt, and insecurity; it can also cause students to have poor performance and withdraw from foreign language learning (Guy and Radnovsky, 2001; Marcos-Llinas and Garau, 2009; Saito and Samimy, 1996). Students' native languages can also cause debilitating anxiety; however, it can be very difficult for students to break away from the use of their native languages because that's the tool that enables them to ask for assistance, express their frustrations, argue a point, explain an idea, and socialize (Duxbury and Tsai, 2010).

Language-skill-specific anxiety refers to listening, speaking, reading, and writing anxiety in the learning of a foreign language. In general, students who struggle with anxiety are more likely to struggle with reading, writing, and most notably, listening comprehension and speaking (Cheng, Horwitz, and Shallert, 1999; Vogely, 1998; Young, 1986, 1992). Research shows that students, regardless of anxiety within a specific category of *language-skill-specific anxiety*, tend to have a general feeling of low-self confidence (Cheng et al., 1999). Students experiencing *language-skill-specific anxiety* have reported that a foreign language class moves too quickly and they feel left behind, and therefore, they require more time for their studies (MacIntyre and Gardner, 1991). Many learners have also expressed a belief that in order to be "good" at a foreign language, they need to have perfect pronunciation, large vocabulary, extensive grammar knowledge, overseas experience, and a natural aptitude for language before they even open their mouths (Vogely, 1998). Speaking in class seems to be the most troublesome area for students learning a foreign language (Young, 1992). Students feel less uncomfortable for a speaking drill or a prepared speech, but very anxious when they are called on unexpectedly or to role-play in front of the rest of their peers (Young, 1986). Furthermore, students learning a foreign language have also expressed challenges in and struggles with discriminating certain sounds and structures in the foreign language. Situations that are most challenging involve large class discussions where multiple people are responding quickly (Horowitz et al., 1986). In addition, students learning a foreign language experience reading and writing anxiety, which are associated adversely with their reading and writing processes and performance in that language (Cheng, 2002; Mills, Pajares, and Herron, 2006; Lin and Ho, 2009).

Related to *foreign language anxiety* and *language-skill-specific anxiety*, and fairly recently identified as distinguished from other forms of anxiety, is *foreign language classroom anxiety*[2] (FLCA) (von Wörde, 1998). FLCA is a more general type of anxiety in learning a foreign language with a strong speaking anxiety element and “low self-confidence” is identified as an important component of FLCA construct (Cheng et al., 1999). Research also indicates that FLCA is a complex, multi-dimensional phenomenon (Young, 1992). There are many potential sources of learners’ anxiety in the foreign language classrooms (Bailey, 1983; Garrett and Young, 2009; Horwitz, 2001; Horwitz and Young, 1991; Lucas, 1984; Yan and Horwitz, 2008). FLCA interferes with the acquisition, retention, and production of the new language (MacIntyre and Gardner, 1991; Saito and Samimy, 1996).

ANXIETY IN LANGUAGE ACQUISITION THEORIES AND TEACHING METHODS AND APPROACHES

There are a number of important SLA theories (see Baker, 1993; McLaughlin, 1987). The work most often cited and discussed is that of

[2] Terms foreign language classroom anxiety (FLCA) and anxiety in foreign language classrooms are used interchangeably in the book.

Krashen (Echevarria and Graves, 2007). Krashen's (1982, 1985, 1994) monitor model becomes a very important SLA theory, although it is most widely debated (Echevarria and Graves, 2007). There are five hypotheses comprising this theory: The Acquisition-Learning Hypothesis, the Natural Order Hypothesis, the Monitor Hypothesis, the Input Hypothesis, and the Affective Filter Hypothesis (Krashen, 1982, 1985, 1994).

Anxiety is clearly related to the Affective Filter Hypothesis. According to Krashen (1982, 1985, 1994), learners often develop mental blocks that hider the acquisition of the language. He explained these blocks with the Affective Filter Hypothesis, which is related to the emotional side of language use. It relates to "such aspects as attitude, anxiety, motivation, and self-confidence" (Echevarria and Graves, 2007, p. 44). The assumption of this hypothesis is that when the filter is up, as one is anxious, that acquisition cannot occur (von Wörde, 1998). In other words, if the learner is anxious or lacks self-confidence, these affective variables can block or impede the learning of a second language (Echevarria and Graves, 2007). This hypothesis suggests that a positive affective learning environment enhances language learning. Although Krashen's Affective Filter Hypothesis has received several criticisms, e.g., "the pedagogic proposals are not fully supported" (Ellis, 1990, p. 60), it provides "a coherent set of ideas firmly grounded in L2 acquisition research" (p. 60). It is suggested that second or foreign language teaching methods and approaches set "creating a stress free environment" as one objective; and language teachers make sure that their classroom learning environments are as stress free as possible (Echevarria and Graves, 2007).

Looking back on the history of foreign language teaching, the following methods and approaches were developed with "a low stress environment" as one objective: Community Language Learning (CLL), Comprehension Approach, and Suggestopedia (Ma and Huang, 1992; von Wörde, 1998). The CLL is based upon the more general Counseling-Learning approach to adult education developed by Curran (1972, 1976). The CLL calls upon teachers to become skillful understanders of their students as whole persons. Becoming a skillful understander means recognizing and accepting the struggles students face as they attempt to internalize another language. The four principles guiding the CLL are: 1) Students are whole persons; 2) students learn best when they feel secure in a relaxed atmosphere; 3) students should have the opportunity to generate the language they wish to learn; and 4) the teacher should "understand" what the students are feeling (Ma and Huang, 1992). The CLL stresses the need to reduce anxiety in the language-learning process. The CLL is a learner-centered approach and characterized by security and group support, which are believed to lighten emotional barriers like anxiety and to intensify language learning (Samimy and Rardin, 1994).

The Comprehension Approach, as the name suggests, places value on students' understanding of the target language and thus emphasizes the listening skill (Ma and Huang, 1992). Psychologist Asher's method, the Total Physical Response (TPR) is one example of the Comprehension Approach. Asher (1977) bases his method on the observation that a baby spends many months listening to the people around it long before it ever says a word. The child has the time to try to make sense out of the sounds it hears. No one tells the baby that it must speak. The child chooses to speak when it is ready. Moreover, according to Asher (1977), much of the linguistic input directed to the child contains commands. The following four principles are guiding the TPR: 1) Meaning in the target language can often be conveyed through actions; 2) retention is enhanced when learners respond physically; 3) feelings of success and low anxiety facilitate learning; and 4) listening comprehension comes first, and students will speak when they are ready (Ma and Huang, 1992).

In addition, the Natural Approach, which was developed by Terrell (1982) and based on Krashen's (1982) theories of SLA, is another example of the Comprehension Approach. It has been widely used to teach Spanish, French, German, and English as foreign languages in North America. The six guiding principles of the Natural Approach are: 1) Comprehension precedes production; 2) speech emerges in stages; 3) speech emergence is characterized by grammatical errors; 4) group work encourages speech; 5) students acquire language only in a low-anxiety environment; and 6) the goal is proficiency in communication skills (von Wörde, 1998).

Lastly, Suggestopedia, which was developed by Lozanov (1979), rests on the principle that the brain is more receptive in relaxed concentration, free of anxiety, and therefore able to take large masses of information that might otherwise be blocked out (von Wörde, 1998). Lozanov (1979) believes that learners set up psychological barriers to learning. Learners fear that they will be unable to perform, or that they will be limited in their ability to learn, or that they will even fail. The reason is that foreign language learners do not use the full mental powers that they have. In order to make better use of their mental reserves, the limitations they think they have need to be "desuggested" (Ma and Huang, 1992). Suggestopedia, the application of the study of suggestion to pedagogy, has been developed to help students believe that they can be successful and, thus, to help them overcome the barriers to learning.

The following four principles are guiding Suggestopedia: 1) Learning is facilitated in a pleasant and comfortable environment; 2) the more confident the students feel, the better they will learn; 3) communication takes place on two planes and learning is enhanced when there is a unity between them; and 4) the means of activating the material should be varied and playful (Ma and Huang, 1992).

The CLL, the Comprehension Approach, including the TPR and the Natural Approach, and Suggestopedia, all emphasize the importance of creating a low anxiety environment for students to learn a foreign language. The developers of these methods strongly believe that a low-anxiety classroom environment can facilitate students' learning of a foreign language in the classroom.

UNDERSTANDING ANXIETY IN FOREIGN LANGUAGE CLASSROOMS

As mentioned above, FLCA is a more general type of anxiety in learning a foreign language with a strong speaking anxiety element, and low self-confidence is identified as an important component of FLCA construct (Cheng et al., 1999). FLCA is often recurring in nature; students who do poorly in the language classroom tend to become more anxious over time (Abu-Rabia, 2004). Anxiety in foreign language classrooms can be caused by several factors; it affects many aspects of foreign language learning; and therefore, its impact should be reduced and/or minimized to facilitate students' foreign language learning in the classroom (Donley 1999; Horwitz et al., 1986; MacIntyre and Gardner, 1991; Saito and Samimy, 1996; Young, 1991).

Multiple Sources of FLCA

As von Wörde (1998) commented, FLCA comes from multiple sources. Some are associated with the student, the teacher, and the instructional methods. FLCA may also originate in low self-esteem, specious beliefs regarding the learning of a foreign language, negative experience associated with the foreign language or culture, or the general experience of foreign language learning. Empirical studies have identified the following specific causes of FLCA: students' fear of speaking and being called on, their fear of negative evaluation, their self-perceived foreign language abilities, their personal learning styles, teachers' classroom teaching methods, competitiveness, unrealistic beliefs, native language problems, and testing (Allen and Herron; 2003; Donley 1999; Horwitz et al., 1986; Kitano, 2001; MacIntyre and Gardner, 1991; Tittle, 1997; Young, 1991; von Wörde, 1998; Xie, Leong, and Feng, 2008).

For example, students' fear of speaking and being called on is a major source of their FLCA. If students are nervous about being called upon in the classroom, as well as having to speak the language in front of the class, FLCA can be said to have occurred (Young, 1991). This type of anxiety stems from "personal and interpersonal anxieties, learner beliefs about language learning, instructor beliefs about language teaching, instructor-learner interactions, classroom procedures and language testing" (p. 427). Students may have a preconceived FLCA towards learning a new language or they may feel uncomfortable in the classroom environment due to the teacher or other students in the class (Young, 1991). This could also pertain to the fact that students may not feel comfortable speaking their own language in public, let alone one in which they are not confident. There is a fear of what others will think of them if mistakes occur while speaking; and they may feel frustrated or annoyed when they cannot express their feelings and ideas using the new language (Young, 1991).

Furthermore, students' FLCA can be related to multiple factors when they are learning the new language in the classroom, including the fear of their non-native accents being ridiculed or even the teacher's error—when correcting the students, it may be harsh in nature (Cheng et al., 1999). Learners who are just becoming familiar with a new language may become nervous, overwhelmed, and frustrated in the classroom (Donley, 1999; Horwitz et al., 1986). This is because they may not understand what they hear, when other students can understand what is being said without much difficulty. It may be hard for the language learners to comprehend what is said if the new language is spoken too quickly or in great length. The language learners may also feel that they must interpret every word in order to understand it as a whole; therefore they spend most of their time trying to decipher what is being said before they can complete anything else. These students may feel isolated and frustrated as well because they do not understand the information being given to them the same way their peers can comprehend and understand (Donley, 1999; Horwitz et al., 1986).

With regards to speaking, as argued by Young (1990), the fear of speaking in a foreign language may be related to multiple psychological constructs including self-esteem, social anxiety, and communication apprehension. By administering a questionnaire to 135 beginning-level Spanish students at a university and 109 high school students, Young (1990) reported that speaking in the foreign language is not exclusively the source of FLCA, rather speaking in front of the class is. Students favored a relaxed instructor, warm classroom environment, positive error correction, partner/group work, and interesting topics for discussion (Young, 1990).

In addition, testing can be another source of students' FLCA (Donley, 1999; MacIntyre and Gardner, 1991; Madsen, 1982). If they "…worry over the frequent testing and examinations in a language classroom" (MacIntyre and Gardner, 1991, p. 105), FLCA can occur. Similarly, a fear of failure on foreign language exams also causes FLCA (MacIntyre and Gardner, 1991). Nervousness about tests, as argued by Donley (1999), is part of many students' experience of learning a foreign language. Nervousness can stem from diligent studying and insufficient results or unfamiliarity with the test format or if the student is tested on information that was not presented to him or her in the classroom. If a student is learning a new language and then is being tested on information that is presented in a non-native language, it can create much anxiety. The student may not know the answers to the questions, let alone understand what the test is asking of him or her (Donley, 1999).

Impact of FLCA on Learning

Research has shown that FLCA can have a widespread influence on cognitive, affective, and behavioral functioning in the process of foreign language learning (Andrade, and Williams, 2009; Chen, and Chang, 2009; Cubukcu, 2008; Frantzen, and Magnan, 2005; Fukai, 2000; Ganschow, and Sparks, 1996; Kim, 1998, 2001, 2010; Liu, 2006; Mills, Pajares, and Herron, 2007; Piniel, 2006; Sheen, 2008). Overall, the most commonly affected areas include communication apprehension, reading comprehension, speaking abilities, communicative skills, listening skills, and writing skills (Bailey, Daley, and Onwuegbuzie, 1999; Gan, Humphreys, and Hamp-Lyons, 2004; Huang, 1998; Liu and Jackson, 2008; MacIntyre and Gardner, 1989; Saito et al., 1999; Sellers, 2000; Tallon, 2009; Truitt, 1995; Wu, 2010; Young, 1986, 1990).

Several studies have focused on the examination of language learners' difficulties that are caused by FLCA and related to their oral performances (MacIntyre and Gardner, 1989; Young, 1986, 1990; Yashima, 2002). For example, Young (1986) indicated that FLCA may affect the quality of an individual's communication or willingness to communicate (WTC). WTC, according to MacIntyre (2007), can serve as both an individual difference factor facilitating L2 acquisition and a nonlinguistic outcome of the language-learning process. It also integrates motivational processes with communication competencies and perceived self-confidence.

Liu and Jackson (2008) further studied WTC and FLCA experienced by 547 freshmen non-English major students at a Chinese university. They reported that students who were more scared of being negatively evaluated were also more apprehensive of and less confident in speaking English in front of others and were more anxious about English tests and classroom performance. The "more risk-taking or sociable a student was, the higher the self-reported rating of proficiency in English reading, writing, listening, and speaking, with speaking ability being the most positively related to the LCR [the Language Class Risk-Taking Scale] and LCS [the Language Class Sociability Scale] scales" (p.79). Students who were more sociable or risk-taking contacted their English-speaking friends by writing more and were also more willing to participate in interpersonal conversations.

Further, FLCA might affect students' reading comprehension and writing performance (Cheng, 2002; Cheng et al., 1999; Ipek, 2009; Lin and Ho, 2009; Saito et al., 1999; Sellers, 2000). "Reading in any language is a cognitively demanding process, involving minimally the coordination of attention, memory, perception, and comprehension processes. The reading process is further complicated in the second language, where there are additional factors to be considered such as language ability, cultural backgrounds, and learner motivation" (Sellers, 2000, p. 513). Saito et al. (1999) argued that although reading might seem least likely to cause anxiety because it is usually done privately and provides the opportunity to reflect, two aspects may have great potential for causing anxiety: unfamiliar scripts and writing systems and unfamiliar cultural material. Sellers (2000) further indicated that learners with higher levels of FLCA also tended to have higher levels of foreign language reading anxiety; highly anxious students tended to recall overall less passage content than those students who claimed to be less anxious; and highly anxious readers were more distracted by interfering thoughts and were less able to focus on the task at hand, which ultimately affected their comprehension of the reading passage.

Generally, FLCA also affect language learners' writing processes and performances in the language. Writing is an emotional as well as cognitive activity (Cheng, 2002). Cheng et al. (1999) studied 433 English major students at four universities in Taiwan and indicated that negative self-perception of language competence played an important role in the Taiwanese learners' experiences of FLCA and foreign language writing anxiety. Lin and Ho (2009) further commented that students may become emotionally, physically, or intellectually blocked in writing due to anxiety caused by time limitation, evaluation, peer competition, disengaging subjects, self-perceptions, and uniformed writing formats.

Similarly, FLCA might affect students' listening comprehension in the foreign language (Elkhafaifi, 2005; Kim, 2000; Vogely, 1998). For example, by studying 233 students enrolled in Arabic language programs at six U.S. universities at both the undergraduate and graduate levels, Elkhafaifi (2005) reported that students with higher levels of FLCA tended to have higher levels of listening anxiety; and there was a negative correlation between anxiety and student achievement and a significant negative correlation between listening anxiety and the final listening comprehension grade. Vogely (1998) further indicated that some of the characteristics associated with listening comprehension anxiety are nature of speech, level of difficulty, lack of clarity, lack of visual support, and lack of repetition. Language learners' inappropriate strategies, lack of processing time, lack of practice, environment, tests, the instructor's personality, and fear of failure contribute to their anxiety.

Finally, the impact of FLCA on learning extends beyond the classroom itself. Research has shown that high levels of FLCA may cause a student to drop the language class, switch majors, or never use the language again, which is detrimental to the individual and the education system (Dewaele, 2007). There are also economic and political consequences associated with FLCA. In many countries, multilingualism is a prerequisite for high-paying jobs with better benefits, and the ability to use a second language is considered a sign of goodwill towards others (Dewaele, 2007).

Reducing Anxiety in Foreign Language Classrooms

It is believed that FLCA has a debilitating effect on learners' learning of a foreign language, and both students and teachers should be responsible for reducing anxiety in foreign language classrooms (Abu-Rabia, 2004; Casado and Dereshiwsky, 2001; Chen and Chang, 2004; Donley, 1996; Ewald, 2007; Huang, Eslami, and Hu, 2010; Imai, 2010; Kim, 2009; Lucas, 1984; Naughton, 2006; Nakatani, 2010; Onwuegbuzie, Bailey, and Daley, 1997; Saito and Samimy, 1996; Semmar, 2010; Yan and Horwitz, 2008; Young, 1990, 1991;

Zhao, 2007). For example, as Young (1991) pointed out, it is important for students to recognize their FLCA and share with their foreign language teachers so that together they can come up with a solution to it. Semmar (2010) further indicated that students have certain things to do in order to reduce their FLCA level. First, they should be aware of the types of anxiety they face in the foreign language classrooms and try to reduce their FLCA in order to manage and take control of their foreign language learning. Second, they should become familiar with their own language-learning styles and find ways to reduce their FLCA. Third, organizing support groups for students who experience high levels of FLCA so that they can learn about the experiences, concerns and challenges they face in their foreign language classrooms.

At the same time, foreign language teachers should find ways to alleviate their students' FLCA. Lucas (1984) suggested that teachers employ instruction strategies that facilitate students' foreign language learning in the classroom. For example, the teachers need to create a warm, easy-going atmosphere in the classroom so that students are relaxed and feel less anxious about learning the language. Casado and Dereshiwsky (2001) proposed that foreign language teachers should provide meaningful content that is parallel to students' particular disciplines. The content of foreign language programs should be "systematic, accurate, and empirical measures of students' needs and of the language required by the tasks they must perform outside of the classroom" (p. 550) and in their future field.

Young (1999) indicated that teachers should have students write their fears on the board and verbalize them with the class. This will allow the students to see that other students in the class have anxiety as well. It will help them feel more comfortable in the classroom to know that other students are also nervous. Allowing students to chart their anxiety is another way to reduce their stress and nervousness about learning a new language. This allows the students to see when they are anxious and what causes the anxiousness. Students will also be able to see what makes them feel comfortable and less anxious, allowing them to come up with techniques to cope with their nervousness and anxiety. An activity that can help students reduce anxiety, according to Young (1999), is role-playing. If students are able to act out or give advice to students in situations that cause anxiety, they will be able to gain a deeper understanding of their own anxiety. This also will help students feel support from their peers and teacher, creating a comfortable, relaxing environment. It is also very important for teachers to offer positive reinforcement when students have succeeded in order to build the student's confidence.

CONCLUSION

To conclude, this chapter described what anxiety is in foreign language classrooms and how it affects learners in learning a foreign language. It defined, explained, and differentiated key terms related to anxiety in foreign language classrooms. It described and discussed anxiety by locating it in language acquisition theories and teaching methods. This chapter also discussed what factors cause FLCA, how it affects language learning, and the implications of how the debilitating effects of FLCA on learning can be reduced in foreign language classrooms. As suggested by many researchers in the field (Noormohamadi, 2009; Oya, Manalo, and Greenwood, 2004), continued research in FLCA is extremely important because it helps teachers and students connect their passion to teach and learn a foreign language in a stress-free classroom environment.

REFERENCES

Abu-Rabia, S. (2004). Teachers' roles, learners' gender differences, and FL anxiety among seventh-grade students studying English as a FL. *Educational Psychology, 24*(5), 711-721.

Aida, Y. (1994). Examination of Horwitz, Horwitz, and Cope's construct of foreign language anxiety: The case of students of Japanese. *The Modern Language Journal, 78*, 155–168.

Allen, H. W., and Herron, C. (2003). A mixed-methodology investigation of the linguistic and affective outcomes of summer study abroad. *Foreign Language Annals, 36*(3), 370-385.

Andrade, M., and Williams, K. (2009). Foreign language learning anxiety in Japanese EFL university classes: Physical, emotional, expressive, and verbal reactions. *Sophia Junior College Faculty Journal, 29*, 1-24.

Asher, J. (1977). *Learning another language through actions: The complete teacher's guidebook*. Los Gatos, CA: Sky Oaks Productions.

Bailey, K. M. (1983). Competitiveness and anxiety in adult second language learning: Looking at and through the diary studies. In H. W. Seliger and M. H. Long (Eds.), *Classroom-oriented research in second language acquisition*. Rowley, MA: Newbury House.

Bailey, P., Daley, C. E., and Onwuegbuzie, A. J. (1999). Foreign language anxiety and learning style. *Foreign Language Annals, 32*(1), 63-76.

Baker, S. C. (1993). *Foundations of bilingual education and bilingualism.* Philadelphia: Multilingual Matters.

Casado, M. A., and Dereshiwsky, M. I. (2001). Foreign language anxiety of university students. *College Student Journal, 35*, 539-551.

Chen, I. J., and Chang, C. C. (2009). Cognitive load theory: An empirical study of anxiety and task performance in language learning. *Electronic Journal of Research in Educational Psychology, 7*(2), 729–745.

Chen, T. Y., and Chang, G. B. Y. (2004). The relationship between foreign language anxiety and learning difficulties. *Foreign Language Annals, 37*(2), 279–289.

Cheng, Y. (2002). Factors associated with foreign language writing anxiety. *Foreign Language Annals, 35*(5), 647–656.

Cheng, Y. S., Horwitz, E. K., and Schallert, D. L. (1999). Language anxiety: Differentiating writing and speaking components. *Language Learning, 49*(3), 417-446.

Cubukcu, F. (2008). A study on the correlation between self-efficacy and foreign language learning anxiety. *Journal of Theory and Practice in Education, 4*(1), 148-158.

Curran, D. A. (1972). *Counseling-learning: A whole-person model for education*. East Dubuque, IL: Counseling-Learning Publications.

Curran, D. A. (1976). *Counseling-learning in second languages.* East Dubuque, IL: Counseling-Learning Publications.

Dewaele, J. M. (2007). The effect of multilingualism, sociobiographical, and situational factors on communicative anxiety and foreign language anxiety of mature language learners. *International Journal of Bilingualism, 11*(4), 391–409.

Donley, P. M. (1996). Ten ways to cope with foreign language anxiety. *The Forum of Phi Sigma Iota, 8*(1), 13.

Donley, P. M. (1999). Language anxiety and how to manage it: What educators need to know. *Mosaic, 6*(3), 3-9.

Duxbury, J. G. and Tsai, L. L. (2010). The effects of cooperative learning on foreign language anxiety: A comparative study of Taiwanese and American universities. *International Journal of Instruction, 3*(1), 3-18.

Echevarria, J. and Graves, A. (2007). *Sheltered content instruction: Teaching students with diverse abilities* (3rd ed.). Boston : Allyn and Bacon.

Ehrman, M., and Oxford, R. L. (1995). Cognition plus: Correlates of adult language proficiency. *Modern Language Journal, 79*, 67–89.

Elkhafaifi, H. (2005). Listening comprehension and anxiety in the Arabic language classroom. *The Modern Language Journal, 89*(2), 206–220.

Ellis, R. (1990). *Instructed second language acquisition: Learning in the classroom*. Oxford: Basil Blackwell, Ltd.

Ewald, J. D. (2007). Foreign language learning anxiety in upper-level classes: Involving students as researchers. *Foreign Language Annals, 40*(1), 122–142.

Frantzen, D., and Magnan, S. S. (2005). Anxiety and the true beginner-false beginner dynamic in beginning French and Spanish classes. *Foreign Language Annals, 38*(2), 171–186.

Fukai, M. (2000). College Japanese classroom anxiety: True and false beginners. Paper presented at the Annual Meeting of the Midwest Conference of Asian Affairs, Bloomington, IN. (ERIC Document Reproduction Service No. ED 450 597).

Garrett, P., and Young, R. F. (2009). Theorizing affect in foreign language learning: An analysis of one learner's responses to a communicative Portuguese course. *The Modern Language Journal, 93*(2), 209-226.

Gan, Z., Humphreys, G., and Hamp-Lyons, L. (2004). Understanding successful and unsuccessful EFL students in Chinese universities. *The Modern Language Journal, 88*(2), 229-244.

Ganschow, L. and Sparks, R. L. (1996). Anxiety about foreign language learning among high school women. *The Modern Language Journal, 80*, 199-212.

Garcia, C. L. (1998). *Too scared to learn: Overcoming academic anxiety*. California: Corwin Press.

Gregersen, T., and Horwitz, E. K. (2002). Language learning and perfectionism: Anxious and non-anxious language learners' reactions to their own oral performance. *The Modern Language Journal, 86*(4), 562–570.

Guy, S., and Radnovsky, M. L. (2001). Learning language under tension: New directions from a qualitative study. *Modern Language Journal, 85*, 259–278.

Horwitz, E. K. (2001). Language anxiety and achievement. *Annual Review of Applied Linguistics, 21*, 112-126.

Horwitz, E. K., Horwitz, M. B., and Cope, J. A. (1986). Foreign language classroom anxiety. *The Modern Language Journal, 70*, 125-132.

Horwitz, E. K., and Young, D. J. (Eds.). (1991). *Language anxiety: From theory and research to classroom implications*. Englewood Cliffs, NJ: Prentice Hall.

Huang, J. F. (1998). *Students' learning difficulties in a second-language-speaking classroom.* Paper presented at the Annual Meeting of the

American Educational Research Association, San Diego, CA. (ERIC Document Reproduction Service No. ED 420 193)

Huang, S., Eslami, Z., and Hu, R. J. S. (2010). The relationship between teacher and peer support and English-language learners' anxiety. *English Language Teaching, 3*(1), 32-40.

Imai, Y. (2010). Emotions in SLA: New insights from collaborative learning for an EFL classroom. *The Modern Language Journal, 94*(2), 278-292.

Ipek, H. (2009). Foreign language reading anxiety: Proficiency and gender. *The International Journal of Learning, 16*(8), 293-299.

Kim, S. Y. (2010). Is foreign language classroom anxiety context free or context dependent? *Foreign Language Annals, 43*(2), 187-189.

Kim, J. H. (2000). *Foreign language listening anxiety: A study of Korean students learning English.* Unpublished doctoral dissertation, The University of Texas, Austin.

Kim, S. Y. (1998). *Affective experiences of Korean college students in different instructional contexts: Anxiety and motivation in reading and conversation courses.* Unpublished doctoral dissertation, The University of Texas, Austin.

Kim, S. Y. (2009). Questioning the stability of foreign language classroom anxiety and motivation across different classroom contexts. *Foreign Language Annals, 42*(1), 138-157.

Kim, Y. (2001). *Foreign language anxiety as an individual difference variable in performance: From an interactionist's perspective.* Opinion Papers (ERIC, ED, 457 695).

Kitano, K. (2001). Anxiety in the college Japanese language classroom. *The Modern Language Journal, 85*(4), 549-566.

Krashen, S. (1982). Accounting for child-adult differences in second language rate and attainment. In S. Krashen, R. Scarcella, and M. Long (Eds.), *Child-adult differences in second language acquisition.* Rowley, MA: Newbury House.

Krashen, S. (1985). *The input hypothesis: Issues and implications.* New York: Longman.

Krashen, S. (1994). Bilingual education and second language acquisition theory. In *Schooling and language minority students: A theoretical framework* (2nd ed.). Los Angeles: California State University, National Evaluation, Dissemination, and Assessment Center.

Lazarus, R. S. (1991). *Emotion and adaptation*. London: Oxford University Press.

Lightbown, P. M., and Spada, N. (1993). *How languages are learned*. Oxford: Oxford University Press.

Lin, G. H. C., and Ho, M. M. S. (2009). *An exploration into foreign language writing anxiety from Taiwanese university students' perspectives*. Paper presented at 2009 NCUE Fourth Annual Conference on Language, Teaching, Literature, Linguistics, Translation and Interpretation. Kaohsiung, Taiwan.

Liu, M. (2006). Anxiety in Chinese EFL students at different proficiency levels. *System, 34*(3), 301–316.

Liu, M. and Jackson, J. (2008). An exploration of Chinese EFL learners' unwillingness to communicate and foreign language anxiety. *The Modern Language Journal, 92*, 71-86.

Lozanov, G. (1979). *Suggestology and outlines of suggestopedy*. New York: Gordon and Breach Science Publishers.

Lucas, J. (1984). Communication apprehension in the ESL classroom: Getting our students to talk. *Foreign Language Annals, 17*(6), 593–598.

MacIntyre, P. D. (2007). Willingness to communicate in the second language: Understanding the decision to speak as a volitional process. *The Modern Language Journal, 91*(4), 564–576.

MacIntyre, P. D., and Gardner, R. C. (1989). Anxiety and second-language learning: Toward a theoretical clarification. *Language Learning, 39*(2), 251-275.

MacIntyre, P. D. and Gardner, R. C. (1991). Methods and results in the study of anxiety and language learning: A review of the literature. *Language Learning, 41*(1), 85-117.

Madsen, H. S. (1982). Determining the debilitative impact of test anxiety. *Language Learning, 32*(1), 133-143.

Ma, Y., and Huang, J. (1992). *A practical guide to English teaching methodology*. Changsha: Hunan Normal University Press.

Marcos-Llinás, M., Garau, M. J. (2009). Effects of language anxiety on three proficiency-level courses of Spanish as a foreign language. *Foreign Language Annals, 42*(1), 94-111.

Mills, N., Pajares, F., and Herron, C. (2007). Self-efficacy of college intermediate French students: relation to achievement and motivation. *Language Learning, 57*(3), 417–442.

Mills, N., Pajares, F., and Herron, C. (2006). A reevaluation of the role of anxiety: Self-efficacy, anxiety, and their relation to reading and listening proficiency. *Foreign Language Annals, 39*(2), 276–295.

Nakatani, Y. (2010). Identifying strategies that facilitate EFL learners' oral communication: A classroom study using multiple data collection procedures. *The Modern Language Journal, 94*(1), 116-136.

Naughton, D. (2006). Cooperative strategy training and oral interaction: Enhancing small group communication in the language classroom. *The Modern Language Journal, 90*(2), 169-184.

Noormohamadi, R. (2009). On the relationship between language learning strategies and foreign language anxiety. *Journal of Pan-Pacific Association of Applied Linguistics, 13*(1), 39-52.

Onwuegbuzie, A. J., Bailey, P., and Daley, C. E. (1997). *Foreign language anxiety among college students*. Paper presented at the Annual Meeting of the Mid-South Educational Research Association, Memphis, TN.

Onwuegbuzie, A., Bailey, P., and Daley, C. E. (2000). The validation of three scales measuring anxiety at different stages of the foreign language learning process: The input anxiety scale, the processing anxiety scale, and the output anxiety scale. *Language Learning, 50*, 87-117.

Oya, T., Manalo, E., and Greenwood, J. (2004). The influence of personality and anxiety on the oral performance of Japanese speakers of English. *Applied Cognitive Psychology, 18*, 841-855.

Piniel, K. (2006). Foreign language classroom anxiety: A classroom perspective. In M. Nikolov and J. Horváth (Eds.), *UPRT 2006: Empirical studies in English applied linguistics* (pp. 39-58). Pécs: Lingua Franca Csoport.

Rodriguez, M., and Abreu, O. (2003). The stability of general foreign language classroom anxiety across English and French. *The Modern Language Journal, 87*(3), 365–374.

Saito, Y., Garza, T. J., and Horwitz, E. K. (1999). Foreign language reading anxiety. *The Modern Language Journal, 83*(2), 202-218.

Saito, Y., and Samimy, K. K. (1996). Foreign language anxiety and language performance: A study of learner anxiety in beginning, intermediate, and advanced-level college students of Japanese. *Foreign Language Annals, 29*, 239-251.

Samimy, K. K., and Rardin, J. P. (1994). Adult language learners' affective reactions to Community Language Learning: A descriptive study. *Foreign Language Annals, 27*, 379-390.

Sellers, V. D. (2000). Anxiety and reading comprehension in Spanish as a foreign language. *Foreign Language Annals, 33*(5), 512–520.

Semmar, Y. (2010). First-year university students and language anxiety: Insights into the English version of the Foreign Language Classroom Anxiety Scale. *The International Journal of Learning, 17*(1), 81-93.

Sheen, Y. (2008). Recasts, language anxiety, modified output, and L2 learning. *Language Learning, 58*(4), 835-874.

Spielberger, C. D. (1972). *Anxiety: Current trends in theory and research.* New York, N.Y.: Academic Press.

Spielberger, C. D. (1983). *Manual for the State-Trait Anxiety Inventory*. Palo Alto, CA: Consulting Psychologists Press.

Tallon, M. (2009). Foreign language anxiety and heritage students of Spanish: A quantitative study. *Foreign Language Annals, 42*(1), 112-137.

Terrell, T. D. (1982). A natural approach. In R. Blair (Ed.), *Innovative approaches to language teaching* (pp. 160-173). Rowley, MA: Newbury House.

Tittle, M. (1997). *The effects of foreign and second language students' irrational beliefs and anxiety on classroom achievement. Research Report* (ERIC, ED, 411 674).

Truitt, S. (1995). *Anxiety and beliefs about language learning: A study of Korean university students learning English.* Unpublished doctoral dissertation, The University of Texas, Austin.

von Wörde, R. (1998). *An investigation of students' perspectives on foreign language anxiety*. Unpublished doctoral dissertation. George Mason University, Fairfax, Virginia.

Vogely, A. J. (1998). Listening comprehension anxiety: Students' reported sources and solutions. *Foreign Language Annals, 31*(1), 67–80.

Wu, K. H. (2010). The relationship between language learners' anxiety and learning strategy in the CLT classrooms. *International Education Studies, 3*(1), 174-191.

Xie, D., Leong, F. T. L., and Feng, S. (2008). Culture-specific personality correlates of anxiety among Chinese and Caucasian students. *Asian Journal of Social Psychology, 11*, 163-174.

Yan, J. X., and Horwitz, E. K. (2008). Learners' perceptions of how anxiety interacts with personal and instructional factors to influence their achievement in English: A qualitative analysis of EFL learners in China. *Language Learning, 58*(1), 151-183.

Yashima, T. (2002). Willingness to communicate in second language: The Japanese EFL context. *The Modern Language Journal, 86*(1), 54-66.

Young, D. J. (1990). An investigation of students' perspectives on anxiety and speaking. *Foreign Language Annals, 23*(6), 539-553.

Young, D. J. (1986). The relationship between anxiety and foreign language oral proficiency rating. *Foreign Language Annals, 19*(5), 439-445.

Young, D. J. (1991). Creating a low-anxiety classroom environment: What does language anxiety research suggest? *The Modern Language Journal, 75*, 426-439.

Young, D. J. (1992). Language anxiety from the foreign language specialist's perspective: Interviews with Krashen, Omaggio Hadley, Terrell, and Raadin. *Foreign Language Annals, 25*(2), 157-172.

Young, R. (1999). Sociolinguistic approaches to SLA. *Annual Review of Applied Linguistics, 19,* 105–132.

Zhao, N. (2007). A study of high school students' English learning anxiety. *The Asian EFL Journal, 9*(3), 22-34.

Chapter 2

CURRENT RESEARCH ON FOREIGN LANGUAGE CLASSROOM ANXIETY

ABSTRACT

For many decades, anxiety has been studied by psychologists and educators from multiple perspectives, and its impact on cognitive, affective, and behavioural developments is well documented (MacIntyre and Gardner, 1991; von Wörde, 1998). However, as von Wörde (1998) pointed out, only fairly recently has foreign language classroom anxiety (FLCA) been identified as distinguished from other forms of anxiety (Foss and Reitzel, 1988; Horwitz, 1986; Horwitz, Horwitz, and Cope, 1986; Horwitz and Young, 1991; MacIntyre and Gardner, 1989, 1991; Price, 1991; Young, 1990, 1991, 1992). This chapter provides an overview of current research on FLCA by briefly reviewing 30 related studies that were conducted in the last 15 years (1996 ~ 2010). It first identifies and describes these 30 studies on FLCA. It then reviews the research methods used in current FLCA research. Further, it categorizes the major topics investigated and summarizes the major findings of current FLCA research. Finally, this chapter identifies research gaps and discusses directions for future FLCA research.

THIRTY STUDIES ON FOREIGN LANGUAGE CLASSROOM ANXIETY

Although anxiety has been studied for many decades by psychologists and educators from multiple perspectives and its impact on cognitive, affective, and behavioural developments is well documented, FLCA has been identified and studied as distinguished from other forms of anxiety fairly recently (MacIntyre and Gardner, 1991; von Wörde, 1998). This section has identified 30 related empirical studies that were conducted in the last 15 years (1996 ~ 2010). Table 1 is a summary of these studies.

Table 1. A Summary of 30 Empirical Studies on FLCA in the Last 15 Years (1996 ~ 2010)

Author(s) and Year of Publication	Country/ Region of Study	Participants	Foreign Language Learned	Type of Research	Major Data Collection and Instrument(s)	Purpose / Topic of Study
Duxbury and Tsai (2010)	United States and Taiwan	385 university students	English	Quantitative	FLCAS and SAS	FLCA level and effect of cooperative learning on FLCA
Huang, Eslami, and Hu (2010)	Taiwan	158 university freshmen students	English	Quantitative	FLCAS and CLM	Relationship between teacher and peer support and FLCA
Semmar (2010)	Qatar	238 university freshmen students	English	Quantitative	FLCAS	Validation of the English version of FLCAS
Wu (2010)	Taiwan	66 university (English major) students	English	Quantitative	FLCAS and COLTAS	Relationship between FLCA and learning strategies
Chen and Chang (2009)	Taiwan	88 university (non-English major) students	English	Quantitative	FLCAS and CLSRS	Relationship among cognitive load, FLCA and task performance
Kim (2009)	Korea	59 college students	English	Quantitative	FLCAS and AMQ	Stability of FLCA and motivational goal orientations
Marcos-Llinás and Garau (2009)	United States	134 university students	Spanish	Quantitative	FLCAS	Effects of FLCA on foreign language course achievement
Marcos-Llinás and Garau (2009)	United States	134 university students	Spanish	Quantitative	FLCAS	Effects of FLCA on foreign language course achievement

Author(s) and Year of Publication	Country/ Region of Study	Participants	Foreign Language Learned	Type of Research	Major Data Collection and Instrument(s)	Purpose / Topic of Study
Noormo-hamadi (2009)	Iran	46 university freshmen students	English	Quantitative	FLCAS and SILL	Relationship between FLCA and strategy use
Tallon (2009)	United States	413 university students	Spanish	Quantitative	FLCAS	FLCA experienced by heritage students of Spanish
Liu and Jackson (2008)	China	547 university (non-English major) students	English	Quantitative	FLCAS, UCS, LCR, LCS	Unwillingness to communicate and FLCA
Yan and Horwitz (2008)	China	532 university (business major) students	English	Qualitative	FLCAS and interviews	Impact of FLCA and other variables on language learning
Ewald (2007)	United States	21 university (Spanish major/minor) students	Spanish	Qualitative	Questionnaire adapted from FLCAS	FLCA in the context of upper-level language classrooms
Sparks and Ganschow (2007)	United States	54 high school students	Spanish, French, German	Quantitative	FLCAS and tests in native and foreign languages	Effects of FLCA on measures of native and foreign language proficiency
Zhao (2007)	China	115 second-year high school students	English	Quantitative	FLCAS and Language test	FLCA level and its impact on English learning
Piniel (2006)	Hungary	61 Grade 9 students at a grammar school	English, French, German, Italian	Quantitative and qualitative	FLCAS, STAI and interviews	Stability and Sources of FLCA
Frantzen and Magnan (2005)	United States	490 university students	French, Spanish	Quantitative and qualitative	FLCAS, interviews, and open-ended questions	Comparison of true and false beginners in terms of FLCA and grades
Abu-Rabia (2004)	Israel	67 Grade 7 students	English	Quantitative	FLCAS and Language tests	Relationship between FLCA and student achievement
Rodríguez and Abreu (2003)	Venezuela	110 university (English and French majors) students	English, French	Quantitative	FLCAS	Stability of FLCA

Table 1. (Continued)

Author(s) and Year of Publication	Country/ Region of Study	Participants	Foreign Language Learned	Type of Research	Major Data Collection and Instrument(s)	Purpose / Topic of Study
Gregersen and Horwitz, 2002	Chile	78 second-year university students	English	Qualitative	FLCAS and interviews	Relationship between FLCA and perfectionism
Casado and Dereshiwsky (2001)	United States	283 university students	Spanish	Quantitative	FLCAS	Level of FLCA
Kitano (2001)	United States	212 university students	Japanese	Quantitative	FNE, Modified FLCAS and 3 speaking self-ratings	Relationship between FLCA and fear of negative evaluation and speaking ability
Sellers (2000)	United States	89 university students	Spanish	Quantitative	FLCAS, RAS, CIQ, and reading test	Relationship between FLCA and reading in Spanish
Cheng, Horwitz, and Schallert, 1999	Taiwan	433 university (English major) students	English	Quantitative	FLCAS and SLWAT	Relationship between FLCA and foreign language writing anxiety
von Wörde, 1998	United States	15 university students	French, German, Spanish	Quantitative and qualitative	FLCAS and interviews	Causes of FLCAS and ways to reduce it
Onwuegbuzie, Bailey, and Daley (1997)	United States	210 university students	French, Spanish, German, Japanese	Quantitative	FLCAS and SPPCS	Predictors of FLCA
Tittle (1997)	United States	94 university students	Russian, Spanish, English	Quantitative	FLCAS and IBT	Relationship between FLCA, irrational beliefs, and achievement
Ganschow and Sparks (1996)	United States	154 Grades 9 and 10 female high school students	Spanish, French, German, Latin	Quantitative	FLCAS	Relationship between FLCA and native language skill and foreign language aptitude
Saito and Samimy (1996)	United States	257 university students	Japanese	Quantitative	Questionnaire measuring FLCA and other variables	Effects of FLCA and other variables on language performance

The following six observations were made for Table 1. First, current FLCA research has become internationally active. These 30 identified studies were conducted in the following ten countries and regions: United States

(Allen and Herron, 2003; Casado and Dereshiwsky, 2001; Duxbury and Tsai, 2010; Ewald, 2007; Frantzen and Magnan, 2005; Ganschow and Sparks, 1996; Kitano, 2001; Marcos-Llinás and Garau, 2009; Onwuegbuzie et al., 1997; Saito and Samimy, 1996; Sellers, 2000; Sparks and Ganschow, 2007; Tallon , 2009; Tittle , 1997; von Wörde, 1998), Taiwan (Chen and Chang, 2009; Chen and Chang, 2004; Cheng et al., 1999; Duxbury and Tsai, 2010; Huang et al., 2010; Wu, 2010), China (Liu and Jackson, 2008; Yan and Horwitz, 2008; Zhao, 2007), Qatar (Semmar, 2010); Korea (Kim, 2009), Iran (Noormohamadi, 2009), Hungary (Piniel, 2006), Israel (Abu-Rabia, 2004), Chile (Gregersen and Horwitz, 2002), and Venezuela (Rodriguez and Abreu, 2003).

Second, current FLCA research examines both university and high school students' anxiety issues in foreign language classrooms. The participants of 25 studies were university and college students, whereas the participants of the five studies conducted by Abu-Rabia (2004), Ganschow and Sparks (1996); Piniel (2006), Sparks and Ganschow (2007), and Zhao (2007) were high school students.

Third, current FLCA research examines anxiety issues in a variety of foreign language classrooms. In total, seven foreign languages were involved in these 30 identified studies, namely, English, Spanish, French, German, Italian, Japanese, and Latin.

Fourth, the research methods used in current FLCA research include quantitative, qualitative, and mixed (qualitative and quantitative) methods. Among the 30 identified studies, 23 studies used quantitative research methods, three qualitative methods (Ewald, 2007; Gregeren and Horwitz, 2002; Yan and Horwitz, 2008), and four mixed methods (Allen and Herron, 2003; Frantzen and Magnan, 2005; Piniel, 2006; von Wörde, 1998).

Fifth, both quantitative and qualitative data collection procedures were used in these 30 studies. Further, a variety of instruments or procedures were used to measure FLCA experienced by foreign language learners. However, the Foreign Language Classroom Anxiety Scale (FLCAS) (Horwitz et al., 1986) or a modified (e.g., expanded, shortened, or translated) version of the FLCAS was used by all 30 studies as one instrument for data collection.

Finally, the research topics covered in these studies were diverse. The major topics investigated in these 30 identified studies include the level of FLCA experienced by foreign language learners and the effects of gender, major, and language on FLCA (Casado and Dereshiwsky, 2001; Chen and Chang, 2009; Cheng et al., 1999; Duxbury and Tsai, 2010; Ewald, 2007; Kim,

2009; Kitano, 2001; Liu and Jackson, 2008; Rodriguez and Abreu, 2003; Saito and Samimy, 1996; Wu, 2010; Yan and Horwitz, 2008; Zhao, 2007); the effects of FLCA on foreign language course achievement (Marcos-Llinás and Garau, 2009), or language learning (Yan and Horwitz, 2008; Zhao, 2007), or native and foreign language proficiency (Sparks and Ganschow, 2007); the causes of FLCA (Allen and Herron, 2003; Piniel, 2006; von Wörde, 1998; Zhao, 2007); students' responsibilities for reducing their own FLCA (Semmar, 2010; Wu, 2010); teachers' role in reducing their students' FLCA (Abu-Rabia, 2004; Casado and Dereshiwsky, 2001; Chen and Chang, 2004; Chen and Chang 2009; Ewald, 2007; Kim, 2009; Onwuegbuzie et al., 1997; Saito and Samimy, 1996; Semmar, 2010; Yan and Horwitz, 2008; Zhao, 2007); the relationships between FLCA and learning strategies (Wu, 2010), or strategy use (Noormohamadi, 2009), or student achievement (Abu-Rabia, 2004), or language-learning difficulties (Chen and Chang, 2004), or perfectionism (Gregersen and Horwitz, 2002), or fear of negative evaluation and speaking ability (Kitano, 2001), or foreign language reading (Sellers, 2000), or foreign language writing anxiety (Cheng et al., 1999); and the stability of FLCA or validation of the FLCAS (Semmar, 2010; Kim, 2009; Piniel, 2006; Rodriguez and Abreu, 2003).

RESEARCH METHODS USED IN CURRENT FLCA RESEARCH

Although FLCA is a fairly new area of research, a variety of research methods have been employed in the examination of FLCA-related issues; and these approaches can be categorized into quantitative methods, qualitative methods, and mixed methods (both quantitative and qualitative methods are used in one study).

Due to the quantitative nature of analyzing and reporting the FLCAS scores, most studies used quantitative methods (Casado and Dereshiwsky, 2001; Duxbury and Tsai, 2010; Ganschow and Sparks, 1996; Kitano, 2001; Marcos-Llinás and Garau, 2009; Onwuegbuzie et al., 1997; Saito and Samimy, 1996; Sellers, 2000; Sparks and Ganschow, 2007; Tallon, 2009; Tittle, 1997). At the same time, qualitative methods have been used in current FLCA research. For example, interviews and open-ended questionnaires have been used by FLCA researchers such as Ewald (2007), Gregeren and Horwitz (2002), and Yan and Horwitz (2008). Furthermore, due to the fact that there is a complex relationship between FLCA and other variables and its impact on foreign language learning is multidimensional, several studies used both quantitative and qualitative methods to examine these relationships and effects (Allen and Herron, 2003; Frantzen and Magnan, 2005; Piniel, 2006; von Wörde, 1998).

Quantitative Research

Quantitative research is used to collect and analyze data in order to explain or predict relationships or effects (Gay and Airasian, 2003). In quantitative research, the most common forms of data collection include large-scale surveys, questionnaires, and tests. The Statistical Package for the Social Sciences (SPSS) is a widely used computer program used for quantitative research (Gay and Airasian, 2003). Most FLCA studies are quantitative in nature. The following presents the three most recent quantitative studies (Duxbury and Tsai, 2010; Huang et al., 2010; Semmar, 2010).

First, as Duxbury and Tsai (2010) summarized in their study, many factors have an impact on FLCA, for example, students' motivation to learn (Bandura, 1997; Ryan and Deci, 2002), their beliefs about language learning (Gregersen, 2003; Horwitz, 1986), their personalities (Dewaele and Furnham, 2000; Ehrman and Oxford, 1990, 1995), the way a teacher interacts with students (Deci and Ryan, 1985; Vygotsky, 1986), students' backgrounds in the language (Frantzen and Magnan, 2005), and learning in cooperative groups (Johnson, Johnson, and Holubec, 1990; Oxford, 1997; Slavin, 1991). In their study, Duxbury and Tsai (2010) studied whether or not cooperative learning had an effect on FLCA for 385 students in one American university and in three universities in Taiwan. The FLCAS by Horwitz et al. (1986) and the Style Analysis Survey by Oxford (1999) were employed, along with ten questions designed by the authors: Five sought to establish student perceptions of their classrooms' cooperative atmosphere and five concerned students' predilection towards cooperative learning. Using SPSS, both descriptive (i.e., means and standard deviations) and inferential (e.g., t tests, and the Pearson product-moment correlation), statistical analyses were performed to the data obtained from the returned surveys. The results showed no significant correlation between FLCA and cooperative learning at the American university and two universities in Taiwan. However, results from one university in Taiwan showed a significant correlation ($p < .01$).

Further, Huang et al., (2010) examined the relationship between teacher and peer support and FLCA. A total of 158 freshmen students at a university in Taiwan completed three questionnaires: A background questionnaire, the FLCAS (Horwitz et al., 1986) and the Classroom Life Measure. Results of Pearson correlation analysis showed that teacher academic support was the most pervasive variable correlated with language-learning anxiety ($p < .01$), compared to other types of support (i.e., teacher personal support, student academic support, and student personal support). Language learners felt less anxious when they perceived that they obtained more academic support from their teachers.

Although the FLCAS (Horwitz et al., 1986) has been "rigorously validated for internal reliability, test-retest reliability, and construct validity" (Huang et al., 2010) and used by many researchers in the field, Semmar (2010) attempted to validate the English version of the FLCAS in order to gain a better understanding of the FLCA experienced by 238 freshmen students at Qatar University in their English Foundation courses. At the same time, Semmar (2010) examined whether FLCA was linked to gender and English proficiency level. Factor Analysis revealed three distinct types of anxieties related to English language learning: English-as-a-foreign-language (EFL) Communication Anxiety, EFL Negative Evaluation Anxiety, and EFL General Anxiety. Multivariate analysis of variance procedure indicated significant differences for the English proficiency level but not for gender variable.

Qualitative Research

Qualitative research is used to gain an in-depth understanding of specific topics; therefore, fewer participants are involved and the researcher may interact extensively with them. In qualitative research, the most popular forms of data collection include interviews, focus groups, questionnaires, and open-ended questions (Gay and Airasian, 2003). Again, three qualitative FLCA studies are summarized (Ewald, 2007; Gregeren and Horwitz, 2002; Yan and Horwitz, 2008).

First, Gregersen and Horwitz (2002) conducted an interview study to examine the relationship between FLCA and perfectionism. Eight students were selected from a larger group of 78 university students who were enrolled in second-year English language classes in Chile and who were participating in a quantitative study exploring the relationships between perfectionism and

FLCA. This sample consisted of the four most anxious and the four least anxious participants in the larger study according to their scores on the FLCAS (Horwitz et al., 1986). The results show that "anxious learners reported higher standards for their English performance, a greater tendency toward procrastination, greater worry over the opinions of others, and a higher level of concern over their errors than the non-anxious learners" (p. 568).

Until recently, very few studies have explored FLCA in the context of upper-level foreign language classrooms. Ewald (2007), therefore, conducted a study to examine FLCA in the context of upper-level Spanish classrooms through a qualitative analysis of questionnaire data obtained from 21 advanced students of Spanish at an American university, The results indicate that many of these students experienced FLCA in upper-level classes. Students pointed to the key role of the teacher in producing and relieving FLCA.

Most recently, Yan and Horwitz (2008) examined Chinese university students' perceptions of how FLCA works together with other variables in influencing their English language learning. In the study, the FLCAS (Horwitz et al., 1986) was administered to 532 business major students learning English as a foreign language. Six students from four different course levels with varying anxiety levels were then randomly selected for interviews. A 30- to 40-minute interview was conducted with each participant in Mandarin Chinese. Each interview focused on several topics, including genetic and personal characteristics, social and cultural elements, motivation and interest, influence of first language, class arrangements, regional differences, teacher characteristics, test types, anxieties, individual learning approaches, and achievement. The data was then analyzed using three steps: Thematic analysis, generation of affinities or variables, and interrelationship diagraph analysis. Many students strongly believed that there was a great difference in English ability between them and their peers, and some participants expressed concern over their inability to find effective language-learning strategies (Yan and Horowitz, 2008).

Mixed-method Research

Mixed-method research, which involves the collection and analysis of both qualitative and quantitative data, has recently become a popular process in the field of educational research. The benefit of using mixed-method research is that it can help researchers gather a more unified collection of data

(Gay and Airasian, 2003). Similarly, three studies that used both quantitative and qualitative methods to examine FLCA-related issues are summarized (Allen and Herron, 2003; Frantzen and Magnan, 2005; Piniel, 2006).

First, using a mixed method, Allen and Herron (2003) examined both linguistic and affective outcomes of a summer study abroad (SA) program. The purpose of this study was to examine if significant changes occurred in two linguistic factors, oral and listening French skills, and two affective factors, integrative motivation and language anxiety after SA. The participants were 25 American university students enrolled in a summer SA program in Paris. Results demonstrated that French linguistic skills improved significantly and that FLCA and non-classroom language anxiety after SA decreased significantly. Qualitative data analysis indicates that participants faced two sources of language anxiety while abroad: linguistic insecurity and cultural differences.

Further, Frantzen and Magnan (2005) compared true and false beginners in first-semester university French and Spanish classes in terms of FLCA and grades. Four hundred and ninety students completed a questionnaire that included the FLCAS (Horwitz et al., 1986) and open-ended questions. Randomly selected students were interviewed about their experiences in the courses. Statistical analyses revealed that (a) although neither group was terribly anxious, true beginners were significantly more anxious overall and during processing and output stages than false beginners; (b) true beginners expected and received lower grades than false beginners; and (c) significantly more true beginners than false beginners planned to continue studying the language. Comments on one written open-ended question and in the interviews pointed to the key role of the instructor in reducing anxiety.

Finally, using both quantitative method, i.e., using the FLCAS (Horwitz et al., 1986) and the State Trait Anxiety Inventory (STAI) (Sipos, Sipos and Spielberger, 1994), and qualitative method, i.e., using a case study, Piniel (2006) examined FLCA by questioning its stability across different foreign languages among secondary school students and identified major sources of FLCA. Participants were 61 Grade 9 students of a grammar school in Hungary who were learning two foreign languages simultaneously (English-French, or English-German, or English-Italian, or German-French, or German-Italian, or German-English). The results suggest that it is possible that a learner studying two foreign languages simultaneously develops significantly different levels of FLCA. Furthermore, in the case of six students, these results proved to be independent of students' levels of the permanent characteristic of trait anxiety.

MAJOR TOPICS AND FINDINGS OF CURRENT FLCA RESEARCH

These 30 identified studies examined a variety of topics related to FLCA. This section briefly categorizes these topics and summarizes the major findings of each category.

The Levels of FLCA and Effects of Gender, Major, and Language on FLCA

Several studies examined the levels of FLCA experienced by different language learners and the effects of gender, major, and language on FLCA (Casado and Dereshiwsky, 2001; Chen and Chang, 2009; Cheng et al., 1999; Duxbury and Tsai, 2010; Ewald, 2007; Kim, 2009; Kitano, 2001; Liu and Jackson, 2008; Onwuegbuzie et al., 1997; Rodriguez and Abreu, 2003; Saito and Samimy, 1996; Wu, 2010; Yan and Horwitz, 2008; Zhao, 2007). For example, using a shortened FLCAS (Horwitz et al., 1986), Kitano (2001) examined how 212 students' fears of negative evaluation and their self-perceived speaking abilities are related to the FLCA they are experiencing at the Japanese classrooms in two American universities. The results show that there was a positive correlation between students' FLCA and their fear of negative evaluation but a negative correlation between their FLCA and their perceived speaking abilities. Further, the level of an individual male student's FLCA was higher as he perceived his speaking ability to be less proficient, whereas for an individual female student, there was no such relationship between her level of FLCA and her perceived speaking proficiency.

Further, Zhao (2007) examined high school students' English learning anxieties in Chinese EFL classrooms. In total, 115 students from a high school in China were asked to complete the FLCAS (Horwitz et al., 1986). The results show that Chinese high school students indeed experience fairly high levels of FLCA, which plays a debilitative role in their English learning. Further, male students experience higher levels of FLCA than female students.

In addition, it is believed that learning a foreign language as a major or non-major can have an impact on the levels of FLCA. Wu (2010) studied 66 Chinese adult learners of English (all major students) from a university in Taiwan and indicated that these English major students experience high levels of anxiety in the English classrooms. Further, females show higher levels of

FLCA than males. Female participants "become nervous when asked to answer questions in class, especially when they are singled out or have to give a presentation. They worry about their English proficiency and making mistakes in front of the class. But, they feel less anxious when they are in a pair or group" (p. 183).

Onwuegbuzie et al. (1997) investigated the levels of FLCA and the effects of multiple factors on FLCA in 210 university students enrolled in French, Spanish, German, and Japanese language courses at an American university. A battery of instruments was used in the study, e.g., the FLCAS (Horwitz et al., 1986), the Self-Perception Profile for College Students, etc. The results show that 14 variables such as gender, age, academic achievement, prior high school experience with foreign languages, etc., contributed significantly to the prediction of FLCA. Further, freshmen and sophomores experienced the lowest level of FLCA; and the levels increased linearly as a function of year of study.

The Effects of FLCA on Student Achievement

Many studies examined the effects of FLCA on foreign language course achievement (Marcos-Llinás and Garau, 2009), or language learning (Yan and Horwitz, 2008; Zhao, 2007), or native and foreign language proficiency (Sparks and Ganschow, 2007). It is confirmed that FLCA has a debilitating effect on the learning of a foreign language.

For example, Sparks and Ganschow (2007) examined the effects of FLCA on measures of native and foreign language proficiency. The participants were 54 high school students in the United States, who were also followed over ten years and tested with native and foreign language tests. All participants had completed two years of Spanish, French, or German. They were then divided into three groups based on their scores on the FLCAS (Horwitz et al., 1986). The results show that "the low anxious group scored significantly higher than the high anxious group on all native language measures beginning in second grade" (p. 260). Further, the low anxious group scored significantly higher than the high anxious group on all foreign language proficiency and aptitude tests and also achieved higher foreign language course grades. The results also suggest that the FLCAS was negatively correlated with native language measures of reading, spelling, and vocabulary as early as the beginning of first grade.

Further, Marcos-Llinás and Garau (2009) investigated the effects of FLCA on course achievement in three foreign language proficiency levels of Spanish, namely, beginner, intermediate, and advanced. The participants were 134 college students from a variety of degree programs enrolled in 11 courses of Spanish as a foreign language at an American university. Participants completed the FLCAS (Horwitz et al., 1986) and a background questionnaire. Results showed that the levels of FLCA differed across proficiency levels, i.e., advanced learners showed higher levels of anxiety than beginning and intermediate learners. In addition, there was an interrelation between FLCA and course achievement. However, students with high levels of FLCA did not necessarily exhibit lower course achievement in comparison to students with low levels of FLCA, as concluded in previous studies. Furthermore, there was a medium level of FLCA among most participants, with no significant effect on course achievement.

The Causes of FLCA and Ways to Alleviate FLCA

Many studies investigated the causes of FLCA and ways to alleviate it (Abu-Rabia, 2004; Allen and Herron, 2003; Casado and Dereshiwsky, 2001; Chen and Chang, 2004; Chen and Chang 2009; Ewald, 2007; Kim, 2009; Onwuegbuzie et al., 1997; Piniel, 2006; Saito and Samimy, 1996; Semmar, 2010; von Wörde, 1998; Wu, 2010; Yan and Horwitz, 2008; Young, 1990; Zhao, 2007). It is believed that FLCA has multiple causes, and there are different ways to alleviate its debilitating effects on the learning of a foreign language.

About two decades ago, Young (1990) examined FLCA and speaking from the students' perspective. A questionnaire designed to identify sources of FLCA over speaking in the foreign language was administered to 135 university-level beginning Spanish students and 109 high school students. Results show that speaking in the foreign language is not exclusively the source of student FLCA, but that speaking in front of the class is. Furthermore, the instructor's relaxed and positive error-correction attitude can greatly reduce students' FLCA. One way to provide correction input without much anxiety is, as indicated by Young (1990), to "model students' responses, that is, simply repeat the correct version of what the students are attempting to say" (p. 550). Further, the teacher's "positive, friendly and relaxed general attitude toward students" (p. 551) can reduce their FLCA.

About ten years later, Casado and Dereshiwsky (2001) suggested the following four teaching methods to reduce students' FLCA: "Conducting class activities in groups; explaining grammar concepts in beginning and elementary classes in the native, not in the target language; forming support groups for performance-concerned students so they can discuss concerns and difficulties encountered in language learning; using smaller classes to help instructors identify students experiencing anxiety and give them special attention and support" (p. 549).

The examination of the causes of FLCA and the ways to reduce it has received more attention recently. Abu-Rabia (2004) investigated the perceptions of 67 seventh-grade students who were learning English as a foreign language at two religious schools in Israel of how teachers' attitudes impact their FLCA. The results show that teachers' attitudes were negatively and significantly correlated with FLCA. In other words, the higher the students' evaluation of their teachers was as "supportive, encouraging, and understanding" (p. 719), the lower the students' levels of FLCA were. Therefore, teachers should create a supportive and friendly classroom learning environment for students.

More recently, Zhao (2007) reported that, in most Chinese EFL classrooms, "teachers play the role of controller or dominator. Students usually feel nervous or oppressed. Consequently, they lack a free, relaxed environment for English learning" (p. 29). Further, the high expectations of Chinese parents for their children can be an important source of FLCA. Such high expectations usually do not encourage students, but often result in more anxiety (Zhao, 2007).

Most recently, Kim (2009) suggests teaching implications for reducing FLCA. For example, foreign language teachers should "incorporate pair or group work and games into language instruction to reduce student anxiety associated with public performance and improvisation" (p. 154). Further, the teacher could use meaningful tasks and familiar topics in communicative settings because they may contribute to increasing the comfort level among foreign language learners. Finally, teachers could teach students effective strategies to copy with their FLCA.

The Relationships between FLCA and Learning Strategies and Strategy Use

Recently, several researchers examined the relationships between FLCA and learning strategies and strategy use (Noormohamadi, 2009; Wu, 2010).

For example, Wu (2010) examines the relationship between FLCA and learning strategies in the English language classrooms. Sixty-six Chinese adult learners of English (all major students) from a university in Taiwan participated in the study. Results show that the participants experience high levels of anxiety in the English classrooms. They also reported that FLCA has adverse effects on their learning of English. However, the findings reveal that those students who have expended much effort and time studying English tend to use a larger variety of learning strategies more frequently and they feel less anxious when they use English. It is the language instructors' mission to reduce their students' FLCA and accelerate their learning. On the one hand, the teachers need to "create a less threatening atmosphere, to motivate, and to strengthen student confidence" (p. 184); on the other hand, teachers need to teach their students effective language-learning strategies in order to accelerate their learning. However, students themselves should also develop their own language-learning strategies, which can lower their FLCA levels.

Further, Noormohamadi (2009) examined the relationship between FLCA and strategy use. Forty-six freshmen students at two Iranian universities participated in the study. They were asked to complete the FLCAS (Horwitz et al., 1986) for measuring FLCA and the Strategy Inventory for Language Learning (SILL) (Oxford, 1990), a self-report of preferred language-learning techniques. The results show that the more anxious the students are, the less frequently they use strategies. Further, the result showed that among students with high anxiety, metacognitive and memory strategies were the most used, while compensation and affective strategies were the least. Less anxious students reported using metacognitive and social strategies as the most, on the other hand, memory, and affective strategies were used least.

The Stability of FLCA across Languages and Learners

The FLCAS (Horwitz et al., 1986) is by far the most popular and widely used instrument for measuring anxiety in a foreign language classroom (Onwuegbuzie, Bailey, and Daley, 2000). The FLCAS (Horwitz et al., 1986) has been extensively tested for reliability and validity in measuring FLCA and has proven to be a consistent and reliable instrument (Huang et al., 2010; Rodriguez and Abreu, 2003; Saito, Horwitz, and Garza, 1999; Zhao, 2007).

Using the FLCAS, several studies examined the stability of the FLCA across languages and learners (Piniel, 2006; Rodriguez and Abreu, 2003; Saito et al., 1999). For example, Rodriguez and Abreu (2003) investigated the stability of the FLCA across English and French. The participants were 110 preservice teachers from two western universities in Venezuela, who were majoring simultaneously in these two foreign languages. The 110 participants represented a variety of levels within each language. They completed two Spanish versions (one for each language) of the FLCAS (Horwitz et al., 1986). Separate analyses were performed on the full sample and on a restricted sample that included only those students who were at the same level in both languages. The study reported similar findings as Saito et al. (1999). Further, it provided direct evidence suggesting the stability of the FLCA construct across English and French. In addition, the "analysis of psychometric technical aspects of the FLCAS indicated that the scale exhibited high reliability but moderate construct validity" (p. 365).

Piniel (2006) further examined FLCA by questioning its stability across different foreign languages among secondary school students. Participants were 61 Grade 9 students of a grammar school in Hungary who were learning two foreign languages simultaneously (i.e., English-French, or English-German, or English-Italian, or German-French, or German-Italian, or German-English). The results suggest that it is possible that a learner studying two foreign languages simultaneously develops significantly different levels of FLCA.

Identified Research Gaps and Directions for Future FLCA Research

FLCA research is a fairly new research area (von Wörde, 1998). Further, it is a complex and multidimensional phenomenon (Young, 1992). Many factors contribute to FLCA and have different effects on it (Duxbury and Tsai, 2010; Liu and Jackson, 2008). FLCA impacts different aspects of foreign language learning as well (Abu-Babia, 2004; Chen and Chang, 2004). Therefore, several research gaps are identified and directions for future FLCA research suggested.

First, FLCA is an important affective variable that impacts the learning of a foreign language (Ganschow and Sparks, 1996). However, there are other affective variables (e.g., motivation) and student variables (e.g., self-esteem, use of language-learning strategies) that affect the learning of a foreign language as well (Aida, 1994). Although a few researchers have started to look into these variables (Chen and Chang, 2009; Kim, 2009; Saito and Samimy, 1996; Yan and Horwitz, 2008), evidence remains sparse or inconclusive.

Therefore, future research should focus on how other affective variables and student variables affect FLCA and language learning. Understanding the impacts of these factors will help find better solutions for reducing anxiety in the foreign language classroom.

Second, although much research has been conducted on the topic of teacher roles and strategies that should be applied when working with students experiencing FLCA (Abu-Rabia, 2004; Casado and Dereshiwsky, 2001; Chen and Chang, 2004; Chen and Chang 2009; Ewald, 2007; Kim, 2009; Onwuegbuzie et al., 1997; Saito and Samimy, 1996; Semmar, 2010; Yan and Horwitz, 2008; Zhao, 2007), it is such an important topic that research should continue in order to promote the improvement of foreign language learning for all learners (Kitano, 2001). As university campuses continue to be internationalized (Bond, Qian, and Huang, 2003), students will be expected to learn more foreign languages with greater ease and confidence. It is the teacher's responsibility to guide students, especially in high FLCA environments (Lin and Ho, 2009). As reflective practitioners, teachers should consciously examine their own language teaching beliefs to help dispel those beliefs that negatively impact learners (Young, 1991).

Third, many studies effectively utilized the FLCAS (Horwitz et al., 1986); further, it has been translated into many different languages and adapted as needed. It is difficult to find another research instrument that can be used for measuring FLCA. Therefore, the development of additional scales or instruments used for measuring FLCA would be highly beneficial (Sparks and Glanschow, 2007).

Fourth, although most FLCA studies provided sound findings, many researchers consistently suggest that future studies validate current findings by using a larger sample size, wider range of subjects, and different types of language tasks or tests (Chen and Chang, 2009) or more participants and various data sources such as classroom observation and interviews with teachers (Fukai, 2000). In more quantitatively focused studies, researchers often stated that more qualitative data would be useful and vice versa. This is because there are complex relationships among FLCA and other variables and the impact of FLCA on foreign language learning is multidimensional (Allen and Herron, 2003; Frantzen and Magnan, 2005; Piniel, 2006; von Wörde, 1998). What these implications indicate is that future FLCA studies should use both quantitative and qualitative methods to better examine these relationships and the multidimensional impact of FLCA on language learning.

Finally, although a few studies have examined the stability of FLCA (Semmar, 2010; Kim, 2009; Piniel, 2006; Rodriguez and Abreu, 2003), the issue of stability of FLCA will continue to stimulate further research (Rodriguez, 2010). Therefore, future FLCA research should continue to investigate the stability of FLCA across various learners, different educational and cultural contexts, and multiple languages.

Conclusion

To conclude, this chapter provided an overview of current research on FLCA by briefly reviewing 30 related studies that were conducted in the last 15 years (1996 ~ 2010). It first identified and described these 30 studies on FLCA, focusing on the participants, data collection procedures, and the purpose or topic of each study. It then reviewed the research methods used in current FLCA research. Further, it categorized the major topics investigated in current FLCA research and summarized the major findings of current FLCA research. Finally, this chapter identified and discussed several research gaps and proposed directions for future research in the area of FLCA.

References

Abu-Rabia, S. (2004). Teachers' role, learners' gender differences, and FL anxiety among seventh-grade students studying English as a FL. *Educational Psychology, 24*(5), 711-721.

Aida, Y. (1994). Examination of Horwitz, Horwitz, and Cope's construct of foreign language anxiety: The case of students of Japanese. *The Modern Language Journal, 78*, 155–168.

Allen, H. W., and Herron, C. (2003). A mixed-methodology investigation of the linguistic and affective outcomes of summer study abroad. *Foreign Language Annals, 36*(3), 370-385.

Bandura, A. (1997). *Self-efficacy: The exercise of control.* New York: Freeman.

Bond, S., Qian, J., and Huang, J. (2003). *The role of the faculty in the internationalization of the undergraduate curriculum and classroom experience.* Ottawa: Canadian Bureau for International Education.

Casado, M. A., and Dereshiwsky, M. I. (2001). Foreign language anxiety of university students. *College Student Journal, 35*, 539-551.

Chen, I. J., and Chang, C. C. (2009). Cognitive load theory: An empirical study of anxiety and task performance in language learning. *Electronic Journal of Research in Educational Psychology, 7*(2), 729–745.

Chen, T. Y., and Chang, G. B. Y. (2004). The relationship between foreign language anxiety and learning difficulties. *Foreign Language Annals, 37*(2), 279–289.

Cheng, Y. S., Horwitz, E. K., and Schallert, D. L. (1999). Language anxiety: Differentiating writing and speaking components. *Language Learning, 49*(3), 417-446.

Deci, E. L., and Ryan. (1985). *Intrinsic motivation and self-determination in human behavior.* New York: Plenum.

Dewaele, J-M., and Furnham, A. (2000). Personality and speech production: A pilot study of second language learners. *Personality and Individual Differences*, *28*, 355-365.

Duxbury, J. G. and Tsai, L. L. (2010). The effects of cooperative learning on foreign language anxiety: A comparative study of Taiwanese and American universities. *International Journal of Instruction, 3*(1), 3-18.

Ehrman, M., and Oxford, R. (1990). Adult language learning styles and strategies in an intensive training setting. The *Modern Language Journal*, *74*, 311-327.

Ehrman, M., and Oxford, R. (1995). Cognition Plus: Correlates of language learning success. *The Modern Language Journal*, *79*, 67-89.

Ewald, J. D. (2007). Foreign language learning anxiety in upper-level classes: Involving students as researchers. *Foreign Language Annals, 40*(1), 122–142.

Foss, K. A., and Reitzel, A. C. (1988). A relational model for managing second language anxiety. *TESOL Quarterly, 20*, 559-562.

Frantzen, D., and Magnan, S. S. (2005). Anxiety and the true beginner-false beginner dynamic in beginning French and Spanish classes. *Foreign Language Annals, 38*(2), 171–186.

Fukai, M. (2000). College Japanese classroom anxiety: True and false beginners. Paper presented at the Annual Meeting of the Midwest Conference of Asian Affairs, Bloomington, IN. (ERIC Document Reproduction Service No. ED 450 597).

Ganschow, L. and Sparks, R. L. (1996). Anxiety about foreign language learning among high school women. *The Modern Language Journal, 80*, 199-212.

Gay, L. R., and Airasian, P. (2003). *Educational research: Competencies for analysis and applications*. Prentice Hall: New Jersey.

Gregersen, T. (2003). To err is human: A reminder to teachers of language anxious students. *Foreign Language Annals*, *36* (1), 25-32.

Gregersen, T., and Horwitz, E. K. (2002). Language learning and perfectionism: Anxious and non-anxious language learners' reactions to their own oral performance. *The Modern Language Journal, 86*(4), 562–570.

Horwitz, E. K. (1986). Preliminary evidence for the reliability and validity of a foreign language anxiety scale. *TESOL Quarterly, 20,* 559-562.

Horwitz, E. K., and Young, D. J. (Eds.). (1991). *Language anxiety: From theory and research to classroom implications*. Englewood Cliffs, NJ: Prentice Hall.

Horwitz, E. K., Horwitz, M. B., and Cope, J. A. (1986). Foreign language classroom anxiety. *The Modern Language Journal, 70*, 125-132.

Huang, S., Eslami, Z., and Hu, R. J. S. (2010). The relationship between teacher and peer support and English-language learners' anxiety. *English Language Teaching, 3*(1), 32-40.

Johnson, E. W., Johnson, R. T., and Houbec, E. J. (1990). *Circles of learning: Cooperation in the classroom*. Edina, MN: Interaction Book.

Kim, S. Y. (2009). Questioning the stability of foreign language classroom anxiety and motivation across different classroom contexts. *Foreign Language Annals, 42*(1), 138-157.

Kitano, K. (2001). Anxiety in the college Japanese language classroom. *The Modern Language Journal, 85*(4), 549-566.

Lin, G. H. C., and Ho, M. M. S. (2009). *An exploration into foreign language writing anxiety from Taiwanese university students' perspectives*. Paper presented at 2009 NCUE Fourth Annual Conference on Language, Teaching, Literature, Linguistics, Translation and Interpretation. Kaohsiung, Taiwan.

Liu, M. and Jackson, J. (2008). An exploration of Chinese EFL learners' unwillingness to communicate and foreign language anxiety. *The Modern Language Journal, 92*, 71-86.

MacIntyre, P. D., and Gardner, R. C. (1989). Anxiety and second-language learning: Toward a theoretical clarification. *Language Learning, 39*(2), 251-275.

MacIntyre, P. D. and Gardner, R. C. (1991). Methods and results in the study of anxiety and language learning: A review of the literature. *Language Learning, 41*(1), 85-117.

Marcos-Llinás, M., Garau, M. J. (2009). Effects of language anxiety on three proficiency-level courses of Spanish as a foreign language. *Foreign Language Annals, 42*(1), 94-111.

Noormohamadi, R. (2009). On the relationship between language learning strategies and foreign language anxiety. *Journal of Pan-Pacific Association of Applied Linguistics, 13*(1), 39-52.

Onwuegbuzie, A. J., Bailey, P., and Daley, C. E. (1997). *Foreign language anxiety among college students.* Paper presented at the Annual Meeting of the Mid-South Educational Research Association, Memphis, TN.

Onwuegbuzie, A., Bailey, P., and Daley, C. E. (2000). The validation of three scales measuring anxiety at different stages of the foreign language learning process: The input anxiety scale, the processing anxiety scale, and the output anxiety scale. *Language Learning, 50*, 87-117.

Oxford, R. (1990). *Language learning strategies.* New York: Newbury House.

Oxford, R. L. (1997). Cooperative learning, collaborative learning, and interaction: Three communicative strands in the language classroom. *The Modern Language Journal, 81*, 443-456.

Oxford, R. L. (1999). "Style wars" as a source of anxiety in language classrooms. In D. J. Young (Ed.), *Affect in foreign language and second language learning: A practical guide to creating a low-anxiety classroom atmosphere.* Boston: McGraw-Hill.

Piniel, K. (2006). Foreign language classroom anxiety: A classroom perspective. In M. Nikolov and J. Horváth (Eds.), *UPRT 2006: Empirical studies in English applied linguistics* (pp. 39-58). Pécs: Lingua Franca Csoport.

Price, M. L. (1991). The subjective experience of foreign language anxiety: Interviews with highly anxious students. In: E. K. Horwitz and D. J. Young (Eds.), *Language anxiety: From theory and research to classroom implications* (pp.101-108). Englewood Cliffs, New Jersey: Prentice Hall.

Rodríguez, M. (2010). A response to Kim's "Questioning the stability of foreign language anxiety and motivation across different classroom contexts," *Foreign Language Annals, 43*(2), 185-186.

Rodríguez, M., and Abreu, O. (2003). The stability of general foreign language classroom anxiety across English and French. *The Modern Language Journal, 87*(3), 365–374.

Ryan, R. L., and Deci, E. M. (2002). Overview of self-determination theory: An organismic-dialectical perspective. In E. L. Deci and R. M. Ryan (Eds.), *Handbook of self-determination research* (pp. 3-33). Rochester, NY: University of Rochester Press.

Saito, Y., Horwitz, E. K., and Garza, T. J. (1999). Foreign language reading anxiety. *The Modern Language Journal, 83*(2), 202-218.

Saito, Y., and Samimy, K. K. (1996). Foreign language anxiety and language performance: A study of learner anxiety in beginning, intermediate, and advanced-level college students of Japanese. *Foreign Language Annals, 29*, 239-251.

Sellers, V. D. (2000). Anxiety and reading comprehension in Spanish as a foreign language. *Foreign Language Annals, 33*(5), 512–520.

Semmar, Y. (2010). First-year university students and language anxiety: Insights into the English version of the Foreign Language Classroom Anxiety Scale. *The International Journal of Learning, 17*(1), 81-93.

Slavin, R. E. (1991). Synthesis of research on cooperative learning. *Educational Leadership, 48*, 71-82.

Sipos, K., Sipos, M., and Spielberger, C. D. (1994). A state-trait anxiety inventory (STAI) magyar változata. In F. Mérei and F. Szakács (Eds.), *Pszichodiagnosztikai Vademecum 2. rész.* Budapest: Nemzeti Tankönyvkiadó.

Sparks, R. L., and Ganschow, L. (2007). Is the Foreign Language Classroom Anxiety Scale measuring anxiety or language skills? *Foreign Language Annals, 40*(2), 260–287.

Tallon, M. (2009). Foreign language anxiety and heritage students of Spanish: A quantitative study. *Foreign Language Annals, 42*(1), 112-137.

Tittle, M. (1997). *The effects of foreign and second language students' irrational beliefs and anxiety on classroom achievement.* Research Report (ERIC Document Reproduction Service No. ED 411 674).

von Worde, R. (1998). *An investigation of students' perspectives on foreign language anxiety. Unpublished doctoral dissertation.* George Mason University, Fairfax, Virginia.

Vygotsky, L. S. (1986). *Thought and language*. Cambridge, MA: MIT Press.

Wu, K. H. (2010). The relationship between language learners' anxiety and learning strategy in the CLT classrooms. *International Education Studies, 3*(1), 174-191.

Yan, J. X., and Horwitz, E. K. (2008). Learners' perceptions of how anxiety interacts with personal and instructional factors to influence their achievement in English: A qualitative analysis of EFL learners in China. *Language Learning, 58*(1), 151-183.

Young, D. J. (1990). An investigation of students' perspectives on anxiety and speaking. *Foreign Language Annals, 23*(6), 539-553.

Young, D. J. (1991). Creating a low-anxiety classroom environment: What does language anxiety research suggest? *The Modern Language Journal, 75*, 426-439.

Young, D. J. (1992). Language anxiety from the foreign language specialist's perspective: Interviews with Krashen, Omaggio Hadley, Terrell, and Raadin. *Foreign Language Annals, 25*(2), 157-172.

Zhao, N. (2007). A study of high school students' English learning anxiety. *The Asian EFL Journal, 9*(3), 22-34.

Chapter 3

Overview of Two Studies on Foreign Language Classroom Anxiety

Abstract

Several gaps are identified in the area of foreign language classroom anxiety (FLCA) research in Chapter 2. In order to bridge some of these gaps, two empirical FLCA studies were conducted in the contexts of Chinese freshmen university students learning different foreign languages at three universities in Beijing. China is the country with the largest population in the world; and it has a unique educational system and cultural environment (Huang and Brown, 2009). Considering the large number of students learning foreign languages in Chinese universities and little research conducted in this area, it is of great importance to explore the factors contributing to Chinese university students' FLCA; the effects of gender (males vs. females), major (English majors vs. non-English majors), and language (English vs. other Western languages vs. non-Western languages) on their FLCA levels; and the ways to reduce their FLCA levels. The chapter first discusses the rationale and context of these two empirical studies. It then describes their purposes, participants, and the instruments used for data collection. Finally, this chapter describes the data collection procedures, the data analysis methods, and how the results are reported.

Rationale and Context of the Two Studies

As discussed in Chapters 1 and 2, FLCA is related to foreign language anxiety and language-skill-specific anxiety (e.g., listening, speaking, reading, and writing anxiety in the learning of a foreign language) and fairly recently identified as distinguished from other forms of anxiety (Horwitz, 2001; Horwitz, Horwitz, and Cope, 1986; MacIntyre and Gardner, 1991; von Wörde, 1998). It is a more general type of anxiety in the process of foreign language learning with a strong speaking anxiety element, and "low self-confidence" is identified as an important component of FLCA construct (Cheng, Horwitz, and Shallert, 1999). Current research also indicates that FLCA is a complex, multi-dimensional phenomenon (Young, 1992). Many factors could lead to FLCA and have different effects on it (Duxbury and Tsai, 2010; Garrett and Young, 2009; Horwitz, 2001; Horwitz and Young, 1991; Liu and Jackson, 2008; Lucas, 1984; Yan and Horwitz, 2008). Further, FLCA impacts different aspects of foreign language learning as well (Abu-Babia, 2004; Chen and Chang, 2004; MacIntyre and Gardner, 1991; Saito and Samimy, 1996). Therefore, its debilitating effects on foreign language learning should be alleviated.

MacIntyre and Gardner (1991) argue that anxiety develops from pressure or uncomfortable feelings experienced by students in the foreign language learning setting. Any time that students experience nervousness associated with speaking the foreign language in the classroom, they are experiencing FLCA. Research also indicates that students' fear of negative evaluation, their self-perceived foreign language abilities, their learning styles, testing, and teachers' classroom teaching methods can cause FLCA (Horwitz et al., 1986; Kitano, 2001; MacIntyre and Gardner, 1991). Further, Young (1991) argues that competition between students may also lead to FLCA by making students feel insecure and causing them to withdraw from participation due to the fear that other students may have a better answer.

Research indicates that factors such as gender, major, and language may have an impact on the levels of FLCA experienced by foreign language learners (Casado and Dereshiwsky, 2001; Chen and Chang, 2009; Cheng et al., 1999; Clark and Trafford, 1995; Duxbury and Tsai, 2010; Ewald, 2007; Kim, 2009; Kitano, 2001; Liu and Jackson, 2008; MacIntyre and Gardner, 1991; Onwuegbuzie, Bailey, and Daley, 1997; Rodriguez and Abreu, 2003; Saito and Samimy, 1996; Worrall and Tsarna, 1987; Wu, 2010; Yan and Horwitz, 2008; Zhao, 2007). For example, current perceptions of modern language learning reveal that FLCA is predominantly a "female" subject (Clark and Trafford, 1995). However, research has shown that foreign language teachers show a pattern of favoring females over males in the classroom, and that regardless of the teacher's gender, English teachers hold higher expectations for females (Worrall and Tsarna, 1987). Due to the higher expectations, teachers tend to give females more academic advice and career encouragement than males. Therefore, decreased attention and support from foreign language teachers may cause male foreign language students to experience more FLCA than their female peers. Zhao (2007) further points out that Chinese high school female students of English tend to score higher than male students on English examinations, which may lead to higher confidence levels in female students. Such "favorable experiences" (MacIntyre and Gardner, 1991, p. 111), as stated by MacIntyre and Gardner (1991), can lead to a decrease in FLCA; conversely, the lower test scores achieved by the males can lead o an increase in FLCA.

Research also indicates that FLCA has many negative impacts on the learning of a foreign language (Liu and Jackson, 2008; Marcos-Llinás and Garau, 2009; Sparks and Ganschow, 2007; Yan and Horwitz, 2008; Zhao, 2007). Further, FLCA can develop speech anxiety and social anxiety in the foreign language learners (Young, 1991). Speech anxiety is commonly associated with "stage fright, embarrassment, social-evaluative anxiety and communication apprehension" (Young, 1991, p.427). FLCA and speech anxiety can further contribute to social anxiety, where the students are nervous or apprehensive to communicate in the foreign language because of their language skills (Young, 1991).

As a result, current FLCA research has offered several suggestions for both students and teachers in terms of how to alleviate the debilitating effects of FLCA on foreign language learning (Abu-Rabia, 2004; Casado and Dereshiwsky, 2001; Chen and Chang, 2004; Chen and Chang 2009; Donley, 1999; Ewald, 2007; Fukai, 2000; Kim, 2009; Onwuegbuzie et al., 1997; Saito and Samimy, 1996; Sellers, 2000; Semmar, 2010; Wu, 2010; Yan and Horwitz, 2008; Young, 1990, 1991; Zhao, 2007). For example, Young (1991) suggests that students participate in such supplemental instruction as a foreign language in order to reduce interpersonal anxieties towards foreign language learning in the classroom; and teachers ensure that fair tests, which accurately test in-class instruction, are used to reduce testing anxiety associated with FLCA.

Further, most research suggests changes on the part of the foreign language teacher to reduce FLCA by creating a positive, helpful and relaxed classroom environment (Young 1990; 1991; Donley, 1999; Fukai, 2000). For example, teachers can reduce students' levels of FLCA by using pair work and games in the classroom or even by altering the way in which they correct students' mistakes in classroom participation. As Young (1990) stated earlier, since most FLCA comes from speaking tasks where students are put on the spot and required to produce a dialogue and speak in front of their peers with no warning or practice, teachers should avoid singling out students in front of the rest of the class by having them complete speaking tasks in pairs or small groups rather than in front of the entire class (Young, 1990). Expanding on Young's (1991) idea of altering the way in which teachers correct students' mistakes in the classroom, Fukai (2000) suggests that teachers who are helpful and understanding rather than strict when correcting mistakes can help to reduce FLCA among language students.

Fukai (2000) further suggests that helpful teachers, good relationships between students as well as a structured program could help to reduce FLCA among students. For example, by establishing good relationships with peers, language learners are less likely to be critical of each other in the classroom and more mutual understanding can further reduce FLCA. Donley (1999) indicates that FLCA decreases as students become more knowledgeable in the foreign language and could better control their reactions to FLCA. Accordingly, Donley (1999) suggests ten ways to control their reactions to anxiety in the foreign language classroom such as "discussing their feelings, getting enough food and rest, and being prepared for class" (p.17).

In summary, empirical studies on FLCA have been conducted in a variety of contexts in the world. As summarized in Chapter 2, for example, many studies were conducted in the contexts of learning Spanish, French, German, Japanese, Latin, and Russian as foreign languages and English as a second language the United States (Allen and Herron, 2003; Casado and Dereshiwsky, 2001; Duxbury and Tsai, 2010; Ewald, 2007; Frantzen and Magnan, 2005; Ganschow and Sparks, 1996; Kitano, 2001; Marcos-Llinás and Garau, 2009; Onwuegbuzie et al., 1997; Saito and Samimy, 1996; Sellers, 2000; Sparks and Ganschow, 2007; Tallon , 2009; Tittle , 1997; von Wörde, 1998). Further, several studies were conducted in the context of learning English as a foreign language and learning other foreign languages in Taiwan (Chen and Chang, 2009; Chen and Chang, 2004; Cheng et al., 1999; Duxbury and Tsai, 2010; Huang, Eslami, and Hu, 2010; Wu, 2010), Qatar (Semmar, 2010); Korea (Kim, 2009), Iran (Noormohamadi, 2009), Hungary (Piniel, 2006), Israel (Abu-Rabia, 2004), Chile (Gregersen and Horwitz, 2002), and Venezuela (Rodriguez and Abreu, 2003). However, only a few studies were conducted in the context of learning English as a foreign language in China (Liu and Jackson, 2008; Yan and Horwitz, 2008; Zhao, 2007), but no study examined FLCA-related issues in the context of learning other languages in China.

China, a country with the largest population in the world, has a very different educational system and cultural environment (Huang and Brown,

2009). Many foreign languages are being taught at all high schools and colleges and universities in China. English is a major foreign language that requires most students to learn. In addition, other Western languages such as French, Spanish, and German, and several non-Western languages such as Japanese, Korean, and Arabic are all being taught at Chinese colleges and universities. In Chinese universities, students can choose to study a foreign language either as their major or non-major that meets the foreign language requirement by the Ministry of Education in China (Ministry of Education of China, 1999, 2003). Considering the large number of students learning foreign languages in Chinese universities and little research conducted in this area, it is of great importance to explore the factors contributing to Chinese university students' FLCA; the effects of gender, major, and language on their FLCA levels; and the ways to lower their FLCA levels. Accordingly, two empirical FLCA studies were conducted in the context of Chinese freshmen university students learning different foreign languages at three universities in Beijing, China.

PURPOSES OF THE TWO STUDIES

The purpose of the first study was to examine the effects of gender (males vs. females) and major (English majors vs. non-English majors) on the FLCA experienced by 419 Chinese freshmen students at two major comprehensive universities in Beijing. The following three research questions guided this study: 1) What is the overall level of FLCA experienced by the 419 Chinese freshmen students? 2) Are there any significant gender and major effects on the FLCA experienced by these students? And 3) what are these students' perceptions of why they feel anxious in English classrooms and what they and their English teachers can do to reduce their FLCA?

The second study aimed to investigate the effects of gender and language (English vs. other Western languages vs. non-Western languages) on the FLCA experienced by 436 Chinese freshmen students at one major language university in Beijing. Similar to the first study, three research questions guided the second study: 1) What is the overall level of FLCA experienced by the 436 Chinese freshmen students? 2) Are there any significant gender and language effects on the FLCA experienced by these students? And 3) what are these students' perceptions of why they feel anxious in foreign language classrooms and what they and their foreign language teachers can do to reduce their FLCA?

THE PARTICIPANTS

All freshmen students from two major comprehensive universities in Beijing were invited to participate in the first study. Totally, 439 freshmen students from these two universities submitted their responses. Among these 439 responses, 20 were incomplete and considered invalid, resulting in 419 valid responses. Table 2 shows the result of demographic information about the participants from these two universities.

As shown in Table 2, 419 freshmen students from the two universities participated in the first study. Among the 419 participants, 201 (48%) were from the first university and 218 were from the second university. The participants from the two universities were distributed approximately equally. Further, among the 419 participants, 99 (23.6%) were English majors and 320 (76.4%) were non-English majors. The non-English majors were students majoring in mathematics, computer science, engineering, packaging, gardening, and business administration from the two universities. There were approximately three times more non-English major students than English major students. Of the 419 participants, 221 (52.7%) were male and 198 (47.3%) were female students. The male and female participants from the two universities were distributed roughly equally.

All freshmen students from one major language university in Beijing were invited to participate in the second study. Four hundred and forty-seven freshmen students submitted their responses. Among the 447 responses, 11 were incomplete and considered invalid, resulting in 436 valid responses. Table 3 shows the result of demographic information about the participants from the language university.

Table 2. Demographic Information about Participants of the First Study

University	Major	Gender		Total
		Male	Female	
	English	17	22	39
University #1	Non-English	114	48	162
Subtotal		*131*	*70*	*201*
	English	7	53	60
University #2	Non-English	83	75	158
Subtotal		*90*	*128*	*218*
Total		221	198	419

Table 3. Demographic Information about Participants of the Second Study

Language	Gender		Total
	Male	Female	
English	23	148	171
Other Western	23	88	111
Non-Western	51	103	154
Total	97	339	436

As shown in Table 3, 436 freshmen students participated in the second study. Among the 436 participants, 171 (39%) were English majors; 111 (26%) majoring in other Western languages including French, Spanish, and German, and 154 (35%) majoring in non-Western languages including Japanese, Korean, and Arabic. The participants majoring in English and non-Western languages were distributed roughly equally. There were much fewer participants majoring in other Western languages than those majoring in English and non-Western languages. Of the 436 participants, 97 (22%) were male and 339 (78%) were female students. There were three times more female participants than the male participants, which is a real representation of the number difference between male and female students learning foreign languages at foreign language colleges and universities in China.

THE FOREIGN LANGUAGE CLASSROOM ANXIETY SCALE (FLCAS)

An expanded Foreign Language Classroom Anxiety Scale (FLCAS)[1] (Horwitz et al., 1986) (see appendix A) was employed as the survey instrument. The original FLCAS is a 33-item self-report scale designed to measure levels of FLCA. The 33 questions are scored on a five-point scale ranging from 1 (strongly disagree) to 5 (strongly agree). The FLCAS uses the phrase "foreign language," but English or any other language can be substituted in the items (Horwitz, 2008). The FLCAS is tricky to score because some of the questions reflect anxiety and some of them reflect a lack of anxiety. However, a "5" should always indicate the highest level of anxiety and a "1" the least anxiety. For example, for item 3 (*I tremble when I know*

[1] Permission was granted by the author prior to the studies.

that I'm going to be called on in language class) "5" (strongly agree) indicates a high level of anxiety while "1" (strongly disagree) indicates a low level of anxiety. Items 1, 3, 4, 6, 7, 9, 10, 12, 13, 15, 16, 17, 19, 20, 21, 23, 24, 25, 26, 27, 29, 30, 31, and 33 should be scored in this straightforward way. However, some of the items like item 2 (*I don't worry about making mistakes in language class*) reflect a lack of anxiety. For these items, a "5" (strongly agree) would indicate a low level of anxiety while a "1" (strongly disagree) would indicate a high level of anxiety. Items 2, 5, 8, 11, 14, 18, 22, 28, and 32 are called reverse-scored items. For these items, students' responses should be switched as follows: "Fives" should be reverse-scored to "ones," "fours" to "twos," "ones" to 'fives," and "twos" to "fours." Of course, "3's" will not have to be switched. By paying attention to the regular and the reverse-scored items, higher scores on the FLCAS represent higher levels of anxiety. To determine a student's anxiety level, first reverse-score the items that need reverse scoring, then add up their responses to all the questions, finally divide the total by 33 (the total number of questions). Students with averages around 3 should be considered slightly anxious, while students with averages below 3 are probably not very anxious. However, students with averages near 4 and above are probably fairly anxious (Horwitz, 2008).

The 33 items on the FLCAS were designed around the following three categories: communication apprehension (items #1, 3, 4, 9, 13, 14, 18, 20, 24, 27, 29, 33), fear of negative evaluation (items # 2, 7, 8, 15, 19, 21, 23, 31), and general feeling of anxiety (items # 5, 6, 10, 11, 12, 16, 17, 22, 25, 26, 28, 30, 32). The FLCAS has been widely used in a variety of research settings. Further, it has been extensively tested for reliability and validity in assessing foreign language anxiety and proven to be a consistent and reliable tool (Horowitz, 1986).

In addition to the 33 items, the expanded FLCAS used for data collection also included a demographic information section and three open-ended questions, which examined participants' perceptions of why they feel anxious in the foreign language classrooms and their suggestions on what they and their foreign language teachers can do to reduce their FLCA.

Data Collection Procedures of the Two Studies

The data collection procedures of the two studies were very similar. The FLCAS was first translated into Chinese (see appendix B). The Chinese-language version of the FLCAS was then checked through back-translation; and it was finally pilot tested prior to administration. All freshmen students studying English as a foreign language at the two major comprehensive universities in Beijing were invited to participate in the first study. Participants were grouped by gender (males vs. females) and major (English majors vs. non-English majors) for data analyses.

Similarly, all freshmen students majoring in English, French, Spanish, Japanese, German, Korean, and Arabic at the major language university in Beijing were invited to participate in the second study. Participants were grouped by gender (males vs. females) and language (English vs. other Western languages vs. non-Western languages) for data analyses. Other Western languages include French, Spanish, and German, and non-Western languages include Japanese, Korean, and Arabic in the second study.

Data Analysis Methods of the Two Studies

The data analysis methods for both studies were parallel. All reverse-scored items on the FLCAS were switched as previously described so that a "1" would indicate a low level of anxiety while a "5" would indicate a high level of anxiety before data analysis. Using SPSS, the FLCAS data were analyzed at three different levels for both studies.

For the first study, level one analysis involves the descriptive statistics (mean and standard deviation) by gender (males vs. females) and by major (English majors vs. non-English majors). Level two analysis includes *t*-tests performed to examine significant gender and major differences in responding to each item on the FLCAS. Level three analyses include the MANOVA analyses conducted to examine if there were any significant differences in the FLCA experienced by students of different gender and major. As previously mentioned, the 33 items on the FLCAS were designed around the following three categories: communication apprehension (12 items), fear of negative evaluation (8 items), and general feeling of anxiety (13 items). Three summated scale scores were then created by adding together the scores of individual survey items. Due to the fact that there was likely to be content overlap or multicollinearity among the summated scores, MANOVA analyses were employed to test for significant between-group differences (Casado and Dereshiwsky, 2001). Gender was divided into two levels (males vs. females) and major was divided into two levels (English majors vs. non-English majors) as well. Separate ONE FACTOR MANOVAs were conducted to examine whether there were any significant gender and major differences in the FLCA experienced by the students.

Similarly, for the second study, level one analysis involves the descriptive statistics (mean and standard deviation) by gender (males vs. females) and by language (English vs. other Western languages vs. non-Western languages). Level two analyses include *t*-tests and one-way ANOVA, which were performed to examine significant gender and language differences in responding to each item. If there existed significant differences between language groups, a descriptive *post hoc* analysis was conducted to see where exactly the differences occurred. Level three analyses, namely, the MANOVA analyses were conducted to examine if there were any significant differences in the FLCA experienced by students of different gender and foreign languages. As mentioned above, the 33 items on the FLCAS were designed around communication apprehension (12 items), fear of negative evaluation (8 items), and general feeling of anxiety (13 items). Three summated scale scores were then created by adding together the scores of individual survey items. Due to the fact that there was likely to be content overlap or multicollinearity among the summated scores, MANOVA analyses were employed to test for significant between-group differences (Casado and Dereshiwsky, 2001). Gender was divided into two levels (males vs. females) and foreign languages were divided into three levels (English vs. other Western languages vs. non-Western languages). Separate ONE FACTOR MANOVAs were conducted to examine whether there were any significant gender and language differences in the FLCA experienced by the students.

Finally, the open-ended data were analyzed identically for both studies. As previously mentioned, the three open-ended questions on the expanded FLCAS were used examine the participants' perceptions of why they feel anxious in the foreign language classrooms and their suggestions on what they and their foreign language teachers can do to reduce their FLCA. Participants' responses to the three open-ended questions were sorted, categorized, and analyzed according to the recurring themes.

REPORTING OF RESULTS OF THE TWO STUDIES

The results of the two studies are reported in the following chapters of the book. Chapter 4 discusses the effect of gender on the FLCA experienced by the students. Both studies have examined the gender effect and, therefore, gender-related results from both studies are reported in Chapter 4. Chapter 5 discusses the effect of major on the FLCA experienced by the students. Therefore, the findings of the first study in terms of the effect of major (English majors vs. non-English majors) on FLCA are reported in Chapter 5. Chapter 6 addresses the effect of language on the FLCA experienced by the students. The results of the second study in terms of language effect are reported in Chapter 6. The open-ended findings of both studies are reported in Chapters 7, 8, and 9. Specifically, Chapter 7 involves the sources of FLCA; Chapters 8 and 9 discuss the students' responsibilities for reducing their own FLCA and teachers' role in reducing students' FLCA, respectively. Therefore, corresponding open-ended results from both studies are reported in Chapters 7, 8, and 9, respectively.

Conclusion

In summary, the chapter described and discussed the rationale and context of the two empirical studies conducted to examine the FLCA levels experienced by Chinese university freshmen students learning different languages, the factors contributing to their FLCA, and the ways to reduce their FLCA. The purposes, participants, instruments, data collection procedures, data analysis methods, and the reporting of results for these two studies were clearly described and discussed in this chapter. Each of the remaining chapters of this book involves a specific FLCA topic and presents and discusses the corresponding results of these two empirical studies.

References

Abu-Rabia, S. (2004). Teachers' role, learners' gender differences, and FL anxiety among seventh-grade students studying English as a FL. *Educational Psychology, 24*(5), 711-721.

Allen, H. W., and Herron, C. (2003). A mixed-methodology investigation of the linguistic and affective outcomes of summer study abroad. *Foreign Language Annals, 36*(3), 370-385.

Casado, M. A., and Dereshiwsky, M. I. (2001). Foreign language anxiety of university students. *College Student Journal, 35*, 539-551.

Chen, I. J., and Chang, C. C. (2009). Cognitive load theory: An empirical study of anxiety and task performance in language learning. *Electronic Journal of Research in Educational Psychology, 7*(2), 729–745.

Chen, T. Y., and Chang, G. B. Y. (2004). The relationship between foreign language anxiety and learning difficulties. *Foreign Language Annals, 37*(2), 279–289.

Cheng, Y. S., Horwitz, E. K., and Schallert, D. L. (1999). Language anxiety: Differentiating writing and speaking components. *Language Learning, 49*(3), 417-446.

Clark, A. and Trafford, J. (1995). Boys into modern languages: An investigation of the discrepancy in attitudes and performance between boys and girls in modern languages. *Gender and Education, 7*(3), 315–325.

Donley, P. M. (1999). Language anxiety and how to manage it: What educators need to know. *Mosaic, 6*(3), 3-9.

Duxbury, J. G. and Tsai, L. L. (2010). The effects of cooperative learning on foreign language anxiety: A comparative study of Taiwanese and American universities. *International Journal of Instruction, 3*(1), 3-18.

Ewald, J. D. (2007). Foreign language learning anxiety in upper-level classes: Involving students as researchers. *Foreign Language Annals, 40*(1), 122–142.

Frantzen, D., and Magnan, S. S. (2005). Anxiety and the true beginner-false beginner dynamic in beginning French and Spanish classes. *Foreign Language Annals, 38*(2), 171–186.

Fukai, M. (2000). College Japanese classroom anxiety: True and false beginners. Paper presented at the Annual Meeting of the Midwest Conference of Asian Affairs, Bloomington, IN. (ERIC Document Reproduction Service No. ED 450 597)

Ganschow, L. and Sparks, R. L. (1996). Anxiety about foreign language learning among high school women. *The Modern Language Journal, 80*, 199-212.

Garrett, P., and Young, R. F. (2009). Theorizing affect in foreign language learning: An analysis of one learner's responses to a communicative Portuguese course. *The Modern Language Journal, 93*(2), 209-226.

Gregersen, T., and Horwitz, E. K. (2002). Language learning and perfectionism: Anxious and non-anxious language learners' reactions to their own oral performance. *The Modern Language Journal, 86*(4), 562–570.

Horwitz, E. K. (1986). Preliminary evidence for the reliability and validity of a foreign language anxiety scale. *TESOL Quarterly, 20,* 559-562.

Horwitz, E. K. (2001). Language anxiety and achievement. *Annual Review of Applied Linguistics, 21*, 112-126.

Horwitz, E. K., and Young, D. J. (Eds.). (1991). *Language anxiety: From theory and research to classroom implications*. Englewood Cliffs, NJ: Prentice Hall.

Horwitz, E. K., Horwitz, M. B., and Cope, J. A. (1986). Foreign language classroom anxiety. *The Modern Language Journal, 70*, 125-132.

Huang, J., and Brown, K. (2009). Cultural factors affecting Chinese ESL students' academic learning. *Education, 129*(4), 643-653.

Huang, S., Eslami, Z., and Hu, R. J. S. (2010). The relationship between teacher and peer support and English-language learners' anxiety. *English Language Teaching, 3*(1), 32-40.

Kim, S. Y. (2009). Questioning the stability of foreign language classroom anxiety and motivation across different classroom contexts. *Foreign Language Annals, 42*(1), 138-157.

Kitano, K. (2001). Anxiety in the college Japanese language classroom. *The Modern Language Journal, 85*(4), 549-566.

Liu, M. and Jackson, J. (2008). An exploration of Chinese EFL learners' unwillingness to communicate and foreign language anxiety. *The Modern Language Journal, 92*, 71-86.

Lucas, J. (1984). Communication apprehension in the ESL classroom: Getting our students to talk. *Foreign Language Annals, 17*(6), 593–598.

MacIntyre, P. D. and Gardner, R. C. (1991). Methods and results in the study of anxiety and language learning: A review of the literature. *Language Learning, 41*(1), 85-117.

Marcos-Llinás, M., Garau, M. J. (2009). Effects of language anxiety on three proficiency-level courses of Spanish as a foreign language. *Foreign Language Annals, 42*(1), 94-111.

Ministry of Education of China. (1999). *Teaching syllabus for college English.* Shanghai: Shanghai Foreign Language Education Press.

Ministry of Education of China. (2003). *English teaching syllabus.* Beijing: People's Press.

Noormohamadi, R. (2009). On the relationship between language learning strategies and foreign language anxiety. *Journal of Pan-Pacific Association of Applied Linguistics, 13*(1), 39-52.

Onwuegbuzie, A. J., Bailey, P., and Daley, C. E. (1997). *Foreign language anxiety among college students.* Paper presented at the Annual Meeting of the Mid-South Educational Research Association, Memphis, TN.

Piniel, K. (2006). Foreign language classroom anxiety: A classroom perspective. In M. Nikolov and J. Horváth (Eds.), *UPRT 2006: Empirical studies in English applied linguistics* (pp. 39-58). Pécs: Lingua Franca Csoport.

Rodríguez, M., and Abreu, O. (2003). The stability of general foreign language classroom anxiety across English and French. *The Modern Language Journal, 87*(3), 365–374.

Saito, Y., and Samimy, K. K. (1996). Foreign language anxiety and language performance: A study of learner anxiety in beginning, intermediate, and advanced-level college students of Japanese. *Foreign Language Annals, 29*, 239-251.

Sellers, V. D. (2000). Anxiety and reading comprehension in Spanish as a foreign language. *Foreign Language Annals, 33*(5), 512–520.

Semmar, Y. (2010). First-year university students and language anxiety: Insights into the English version of the Foreign Language Classroom Anxiety Scale. *The International Journal of Learning, 17*(1), 81-93.

Sparks, R. L., and Ganschow, L. (2007). Is the Foreign Language Classroom Anxiety Scale measuring anxiety or language skills? *Foreign Language Annals, 40*(2), 260–287.

Tallon, M. (2009). Foreign language anxiety and heritage students of Spanish: A quantitative study. *Foreign Language Annals, 42*(1), 112-137.

Tittle, M. (1997). *The effects of foreign and second language students' irrational beliefs and anxiety on classroom achievement.* Research Report (ERIC Document Reproduction Service No. ED 411 674).

von Worde, R. (1998). *An investigation of students' perspectives on foreign language anxiety. Unpublished doctoral dissertation.* George Mason University, Fairfax, Virginia.

Worrall, N. and Tsarna, H. (1987). Teacher's reported practices towards girls and boys in science and languages, *British Journal of Educational Psychology, 57*(3) pp. 300 312.

Wu, K. H. (2010). The relationship between language learners' anxiety and learning strategy in the CLT classrooms. *International Education Studies, 3*(1), 174-191.

Yan, J. X., and Horwitz, E. K. (2008). Learners' perceptions of how anxiety interacts with personal and instructional factors to influence their achievement in English: A qualitative analysis of EFL learners in China. *Language Learning, 58*(1), 151-183.

Young, D. J. (1990). An investigation of students' perspectives on anxiety and speaking. *Foreign Language Annals, 23*(6), 539-553.

Young, D. J. (1991). Creating a low-anxiety classroom environment: What does language anxiety research suggest? *The Modern Language Journal, 75*, 426-439.

Young, D. J. (1992). Language anxiety from the foreign language specialist's perspective: Interviews with Krashen, Omaggio Hadley, Terrell, and Raadin. *Foreign Language Annals, 25*(2), 157-172.

Zhao, N. (2007). A study of high school students' English learning anxiety. *The Asian EFL Journal, 9*(3), 22-34.

Chapter 4

THE EFFECT OF GENDER ON FOREIGN LANGUAGE CLASSROOM ANXIETY

ABSTRACT

Many studies have examined the impact of gender on learners' foreign language classroom anxiety (FLCA) (Abu-Rabia, 2004; Clarck and Trafford, 1995; Dewaele, 2007; Ipek, 2009; Kitano, 2001; MacIntyre, Baker, Clément, and Donovan, 2002; Zhao, 2007). For example, Abu-Rabia (2004) and Clarck and Trafford (1995) reported that female students showed higher FLCA than male students in learning a foreign language. However, Zhao (2007) reported that male students experienced higher level of FLCA than female students in foreign language learning. This chapter discusses the effect of gender on FLCA. It first briefly summarizes the previous literature regarding the gender effect on FLCA. As mentioned in Chapter 3, both empirical studies included in this book examined the gender effect on the FLCA experienced by the Chinese university freshmen students. This chapter briefly describes the research methodology that both studies used to examine the gender effect. Further, it reports the gender-related results of both studies. Finally, this chapter discusses these results from the two studies.

BRIEF SUMMARY OF PREVIOUS LITERATURE

Many empirical studies have been conducted in the area of FLCA and its relation to gender (Abu-Rabia, 2004; Clarck and Trafford, 1995; Dewaele, 2007; Ipek, 2009; Kitano, 2001; MacIntyre et al., 2002; Zhao, 2007).

Unfortunately, these studies yield conflicting results in terms of the impact of gender on the FLCA experienced by the language learners (Ipek, 2009). While some studies indicate that male students experience higher FLCA than female students and vice versa, others identify no real correlation between FLCA and gender. Most current research supports the notion that female students typically show a more positive attitude towards learning a new language, even going as far as saying that modern languages are viewed as a "traditionally 'female' subject" (Clarck and Trafford, 1995, p. 315). It has also been shown that foreign language teachers tend to favor girls over boys in the language classroom and have higher expectations for female students (MacIntyre et al., 2002). In addition, female students are more motivated by easy assignments and encouragement, where male students prefer challenges in language learning (Abu-Rabia 2004).

Although some studies show that there is no significant difference between male students and female students with regards to FLCA, most studies indicate that significant gender effects on FLCA exist. For example, Kitano (2001) examined how 121 male and 91 female students' fears of negative evaluation and their self-perceived speaking abilit.ies are related to the FLCA they are experiencing at the Japanese classrooms in two American universities. The results show that the level of an individual male student's FLCA was higher as he perceived his speaking ability to be less proficient, whereas for an individual female student, there was no such relationship between her level of FLCA and her perceived speaking proficiency.

Further, Abu-Rabia (2004) studied 67 seventh-grade students studying English at two religious schools in Israel. Most of the students were female; all students came from Jewish religious families, and classes were separated for male and female students. The participants were asked to complete an expanded Foreign Language Classroom Anxiety Scale (FLCAS) (Horwitz, Horwitz, and Cope, 1986), a Hebrew reading comprehension test, an English reading comprehension test, an English creative writing task, and an English spelling test. The results indicated that FLCA was negatively and significantly correlated to students' achievement on all English tests ($p < .01$). Gender and teachers' attitudes were the only significant predictors of FLCA among these seventh-grade students ($p < .05$). Further, 25% of the variance in the results was due to gender; female students gained higher scores on the FLCAS and lower scores on the L1 and L2 tests than male students. Abu-Rabia (2004) explained that these differences may be due to "female students being more sincere and frank than male students" (p. 719) because females were more likely to report openly their feelings of FLCA. In addition, this study was conducted in Jewish schools in Israel, where male students may have greater exposure to English as a foreign language than female students.

In contrast, Zhao (2007) indicated that Chinese male students experience higher level of FLCA in English classes than Chinese female students. In total, 115 second-year high school students from a high school in China, who had at least five to eight years of English learning experience, were asked to complete the Chinese version of the FLCAS. Further, a final exam used to assess students' English achievement as well as a background questionnaire was used for data collection. The results indicated that these students' FLCA levels were high anxiety in English learning; further, male students experienced higher levels of FLCA than females. Zhao (2007) provided the following explanations regarding this difference. Female students experienced lower levels of FLCA because they usually score higher than male students in English exams and therefore are more confident in their abilities to learn a foreign language well. Unlike female students, male students usually score lower in English exams, which leads to less confidence in their foreign language-learning abilities; and consequently, they become more anxious in English classes.

In summary, previous research on gender and its relationship to FLCA still remains inconsistent and inconclusive. Although many studies continue to analyze this topic, there are still too many discrepancies among the research to make any conclusive statements. However, it is believed that continuing research provides important implications for both foreign language students and teachers.

BRIEF DESCRIPTION OF METHODOLOGY TWO STUDIES USED TO EXAMINE THE GENDER EFFECT

As mentioned in Chapter 3, both empirical studies included in this book examined the effect of gender on FLCA. The first study examined the FLCA experienced by 419 Chinese freshmen students at two major comprehensive universities in Beijing. The second study investigated the FLCA experienced by 436 Chinese freshmen students at one major language university in Beijing.

An expanded FLCAS (Horwitz et al., 1986) (see appendix A) was employed as the survey instrument. The expanded FLCAS included the original 33 items, a demographic information section and three open-ended questions. The expanded FLCAS was first translated into Chinese (see appendix B). The Chinese-language version of the FLCAS was then checked through back-translation, and it was finally pilot tested prior to administration.

In order to examine the effect of gender on FLCA, all freshmen students studying English as a foreign language at the two major comprehensive universities in Beijing and all freshmen students majoring in English, French, Spanish, Japanese, German, Korean, and Arabic at the major language university in Beijing were invited to participate in the first and second study, respectively. For both studies, participants were grouped by gender for data analyses.

Using SPSS, the data obtained were analyzed at three different levels for both studies. Level one analysis involves the descriptive statistics (mean and standard deviation) by gender (males vs. females). Level two analysis includes independent sample *t*-tests performed to examine significant gender difference in responding to each item on the FLCAS. Level three analysis involves the MANOVAs conducted to examine if there were any significant differences in the three categories of FLCA, namely, communication apprehension, fear of negative evaluation, and general feeling of anxiety experienced by students of different gender.

Gender-Related Results of the First Study

Gender-related results of the first study are reported in the order of descriptive statistical results, independent sample *t*-tests results, and MANOVAs results.

Descriptive Statistical Results

As described in Chapter 3, four hundred and nineteen freshmen students from the two major comprehensive universities in Beijing participated in the first study. Of the 419 participants, 221 (52.7%) were male and 198 (47.3%) were female students. The male and female participants from the two universities were distributed roughly equally.

Table 4 presents a summary of descriptive statistics by gender, i.e., the mean and standard deviation for responses to the 33 items on the FLCAS by gender. As shown in Table 4, overall, male students had an average FLCA score of 3.29, and female students had an average FLCA score of 3.16, indicating that both males and females are fairly anxious. However, males experienced a slightly higher level of FLCA than females.

Table 4 also shows that, for male students, levels of FLCA were found in responses to 27 items except 15, 16, 17, 19, 21, and 28, with items 2 (mean = 4.22), 10 (mean = 3.94), and 1 (mean = 3.81) having the highest means; for female students, levels of FLCA were found in responses to 25 items except 8, 13, 15, 16, 17, 19, 21, 23, and 30, with items 10 (mean = 3.81), 2 (mean = 3.72), and 22 (mean = 3.65) having the highest means.

Table 4. Summary of Descriptive Statistics by Gender of the First Study

Item	Mean		Std. Deviation	
	Male	Female	Male	Female
1	*3.81*	*3.22*	0.84	0.92
2	*4.22*	*3.72*	0.73	0.74
3	*3.69*	*3.46*	0.72	0.57
4	*3.36*	*3.27*	0.61	0.50
5	*3.49*	*3.58*	0.94	0.96
6	*3.19*	*3.02*	0.87	0.82
7	*3.22*	*3.05*	0.96	0.94
8	*3.07*	2.99	0.87	0.74
9	*3.61*	*3.47*	0.66	0.56
10	*3.94*	*3.81*	0.75	0.74
11	*3.00*	*3.03*	0.89	0.75
12	*3.50*	*3.39*	0.60	0.53
13	*3.01*	2.93	0.83	0.86
14	*3.44*	*3.40*	0.67	0.62
15	2.80	2.73	0.81	0.80
16	2.87	2.84	0.82	0.84
17	2.86	2.63	0.84	0.66
18	*3.25*	*3.19*	0.55	0.43
19	2.65	2.48	0.78	0.60
20	*3.57*	*3.48*	0.64	0.58
21	2.73	2.56	0.74	0.62
22	*3.68*	*3.65*	0.74	0.69
23	*3.11*	2.98	0.98	0.86
24	*3.22*	*3.19*	0.48	0.40
25	*3.24*	*3.01*	0.89	0.86
26	*3.36*	*3.28*	0.58	0.51
27	*3.32*	*3.18*	0.57	0.42
28	2.98	*3.04*	0.82	0.78
29	*3.32*	*3.21*	0.57	0.46
30	*3.05*	2.91	0.93	0.85
31	*3.25*	*3.16*	0.54	0.36
32	*3.15*	*3.05*	0.84	0.77
33	*3.57*	*3.49*	0.63	0.60
Total	*3.29*	*3.16*	0.26	0.21

Items 10 (*I worry about the consequences of failing my foreign language class*) and 2 (*I don't worry about making mistakes in language class*) reflect the highest levels of FLCA for both male and female students. Item 2, as well as items 5, 8, 11, 14, 18, 22, 28, and 32 on the FLCAS, are called reverse-scored items. For these items, students' responses have been switched as follows: "Fives" were reverse-scored to "ones," "fours" to "twos," "ones" to 'fives," and "twos" to "fours." Of course, "threes" were not switched. Therefore, like regular items on the FLCAS, higher scores on these reverse-scored items represent higher levels of FLCA (Horwitz, 2008). However, item 1 (*I never feel quite sure of myself when I am speaking in my foreign language class*) reflects the third highest level of FLCA for male students; and item 22 (*I don't feel pressure to prepare very well for language class*), which is a reverse-scored item, reflects the third highest level of FLCA for female students.

Independent Sample *t*-Tests Results

In addition to descriptive statistical analysis, independent sample *t*-tests were conducted to examine significant gender difference in the FLCA experienced by this group of freshmen students. Table 5 presents the independent sample *t*-tests results.

As shown in Table 5, overall, male students had a significantly ($p< 0.001$) higher average scores of the 33 items than the female students, suggesting that the male students experienced a significantly higher level of FLCA than the female students. As also shown in Table 5, the male students had significant ($p< 0.05$) higher scores for items 1, 2, 3, 6, 9, 12, 17, 19, 21, 25, 27, 29, and 31 than the female students, indicating that the male students experienced significantly higher levels of FLCA in these areas than the female students.

MANOVA Test Results

Finally, MANOVA test was conducted to examine if there were any significant differences in the three categories of FLCA, namely, communication apprehension, fear of negative evaluation, and general feeling of anxiety experienced by students of different gender. Tables 6 and 7 present the results of the MANOVA test.

Table 5. Summary of Independent Sample t-tests Results by Gender of the First Study

Item	Grouping Variable	N	Mean	Std. Deviation	Value of *t*	Significance
1	Male	221	3.81	0.84	6.811	0.000
	Female	198	3.22	0.92		
2	Male	221	4.22	0.73	6.967	0.000
	Female	198	3.72	0.74		
3	Male	221	3.69	0.72	3.658	0.000
	Female	198	3.46	0.57		
6	Male	221	3.19	0.87	2.111	0.035
	Female	198	3.02	0.82		
9	Male	221	3.61	0.66	2.184	0.030
	Female	198	3.47	0.56		
12	Male	221	3.50	0.60	2.042	0.042
	Female	198	3.39	0.53		
17	Male	221	2.86	0.84	3.191	0.002
	Female	198	2.63	0.66		
19	Male	221	2.65	0.78	2.512	0.012
	Female	198	2.48	0.60		
21	Male	221	2.73	0.74	2.500	0.013
	Female	198	2.56	0.62		
25	Male	221	3.24	0.89	2.750	0.006
	Female	198	3.01	0.86		
27	Male	221	3.32	0.57	2.831	0.005
	Female	198	3.18	0.42		
29	Male	221	3.32	0.57	2.159	0.031
	Female	198	3.21	0.46		
31	Male	221	3.25	0.54	2.130	0.034
	Female	198	3.16	0.36		
Total	Male	221	3.29	0.26	5.374	0.000
	Female	198	3.16	0.21		

As shown in Table 6, the four most commonly reported statistical indicators converged to the same equivalent F-value. Also the significant p-value of 0.000 indicates individual between-group differences.

From Table 7, it can be observed that all three categories of FLCA, namely, communication apprehension, fear of negative evaluation, and general feeling of anxiety had significant differences between female and male students ($p < 0.05$). Male students experienced significantly higher levels of FLCA in all three categories of communication apprehension, fear of negative evaluation, and general feeling of anxiety than female students ($p < 0.05$).

Table 6. MANOVA Results Comparing Gender Group on Three Average Summated Scale Scores of the First Study

Test	Value	*F*	Sig.
Pillai's Trace	0.076	11.344	0.000
Wilks' Lambda	0.924	11.344	0.000
Hotelling's Trace	0.082	11.344	0.000
Roy's Largest Root	0.082	11.344	0.000

Table 7. MANOVA Results Comparing Gender Differences in FLCA of the First Study

Variable	Male	Female	*F*	Significance
Communication Apprehension	41.18	39.49	27.237	0.000*
Fear of Negative Evaluation	25.06	23.66	23.526	0.000*
General Feeling of Anxiety	42.32	41.21	10.053	0.002*

*Significant at $p < 0.05$.

GENDER-RELATED RESULTS OF THE SECOND STUDY

Gender-related results of the second study are reported in the order of descriptive statistical results, independent sample t-tests results, and MANOVAs results.

Descriptive Statistical Results

As described in Chapter 3, four hundred and thirty-six freshmen students majoring in English, French, Spanish, Japanese, German, Korean, and Arabic at the major language university in Beijing participated in the second study. Of the 436 participants, 97 (22%) were male and 339 (78%) were female students, representing the fact that there are more female than male students learning foreign languages at foreign language colleges and universities in China.

Table 8 presents a summary of descriptive statistics by gender, i.e., the mean and standard deviation for responses to the 33 items on the FLCAS by gender. As shown in Table 8, overall, male students had an average of 2.99, indicating that they are slightly anxious; female students had an average of 2.84, indicating that they are probably not very anxious.

Table 8. Summary of Descriptive Statistics by Gender of the Second Study

Item	Mean		Std. Deviation	
	Male	Female	Male	Female
1	2.73	2.57	1.10	1.00
2	*3.57*	*3.16*	0.83	1.19
3	*3.65*	*3.00*	1.07	1.18
4	*3.24*	*3.14*	1.11	1.26
5	2.81	2.59	1.18	1.10
6	2.77	2.77	1.08	1.03
7	*3.18*	*3.04*	0.98	1.05
8	*3.12*	*3.22*	1.08	1.00
9	*3.02*	*3.07*	0.99	1.02
10	*3.88*	*3.54*	0.99	1.15
11	*3.39*	*3.21*	0.78	0.99
12	2.82	2.90	0.91	1.04
13	2.51	2.65	0.98	1.03
14	2.89	2.81	1.02	1.05
15	*3.23*	*3.03*	1.08	1.16
16	2.69	2.47	0.97	1.01
17	2.42	2.08	1.02	0.97
18	*3.44*	*3.06*	0.85	0.86
19	2.43	2.14	0.91	0.91
20	*3.28*	*3.22*	1.12	1.09
21	2.60	2.29	1.08	0.99
22	2.92	2.65	0.92	0.98
23	*3.12*	*3.09*	1.06	1.14
24	2.64	2.71	0.99	0.97
25	2.85	2.79	1.01	1.10
26	2.76	2.69	0.99	1.07
27	2.66	2.49	0.93	0.94
28	2.90	2.87	0.96	0.88
29	*3.32*	*3.15*	1.04	1.17
30	2.67	2.63	0.89	0.93
31	2.74	2.42	0.95	0.92
32	2.93	2.91	0.93	0.93
33	*3.39*	*3.45*	0.74	0.86
Total	2.99	2.84	0.37	0.47

Table 8 also shows that, for male students, levels of anxiety were found in responses to items 2, 3, 4, 7, 8, 9, 10, 11, 15, 18, 20, 23, 29, and 33 (14 items), with items 10 (mean = 3.88), 3 (mean = 3.65), and 2 (mean = 3.57) having the highest means; for female students, levels of anxiety were also found in the same 14 items as male students, but with items 10 (mean = 3.54), 33 (mean = 3.45), and 8 and 20 (mean = 3.22) having the highest means.

Item 10 (*I worry about the consequences of failing my foreign language class*) reflects the highest level of anxiety for both male and female students. However, item 3 (*I tremble when I know that I' m going to be called on in my language class*) and item 2 (*I don' t worry about making mistakes in language class*) reflect the second and the third highest levels of anxiety for male students, respectively; item 33 (*I get nervous when the language teacher asks questions I haven' t prepared in advance*), items 8 (*I am usually at ease during tests in my language class*) and 20 (*I can feel my heart pounding when I' m going to be called on in language class*) reflect the second and the third highest levels of anxiety for female students, respectively.

Independent Sample *t*-Tests Results

In addition to descriptive statistical analysis, independent sample *t*-tests were conducted to examine significant gender difference in the FLCA experienced by this group of freshmen students. Table 9 presents the independent sample *t*-tests results.

As shown in Table 9, overall, male students had significantly ($p< 0.05$) higher average scores of the 33 items than the female students, suggesting that the male students experienced a higher level of FLCA than the female students. As also shown in Table 4, the male students had significant ($p< 0.05$) higher scores for items 2, 3, 10, 17, 18, 19, 21, 22, and 31 than the female students, indicating that the male student were experiencing more FLCA in these areas than the female students.

MANOVA Test Results

Finally, MANOVA test was conducted to examine if there were any significant differences in the three categories of FLCA, namely, communication apprehension, fear of negative evaluation, and general feeling of anxiety experienced by students of different gender. Tables 10 and 11 present the results of the MANOVA test. As shown in Table 10, the four most commonly reported statistical indicators converged to the same equivalent *F*-value. Also the significant p-value of 0.023 indicates individual between-group differences.

Table 9. Summary of Independent Sample t-tests Results by Gender of the Second Study

Item	Grouping Variable	N	Mean	Std. Deviation	Value of *t*	Significance
2	Male	97	3.57	0.83	3.153	0.002
	Female	339	3.16	1.19		
3	Male	97	3.65	1.07	4.862	0.000
	Female	339	3.00	1.18		
10	Male	97	3.88	0.99	2.586	0.010
	Female	339	3.54	1.15		
17	Male	97	2.42	1.02	3.041	0.003
	Female	339	2.08	0.97		
18	Male	97	3.44	0.85	3.812	0.000
	Female	339	3.06	0.86		
19	Male	97	2.43	0.91	2.775	0.006
	Female	339	2.14	0.91		
21	Male	97	2.60	1.08	2.634	0.009
	Female	339	2.29	0.99		
22	Male	97	2.92	0.92	2.441	0.015
	Female	339	2.65	0.98		
31	Male	97	2.74	0.95	2.965	0.003
	Female	339	2.42	0.92		
Total	Male	97	2.99	0.37	2.741	0.006
	Female	339	2.84	0.47		

Table 10. MANOVA Results Comparing Gender Group on Three Average Summated Scale Scores of the Second Study

Test	Value	*F*	Sig.
Pillai's Trace	0.022	3.207	0.023
Wilks' Lambda	0.978	3.207	0.023
Hotelling's Trace	0.022	3.207	0.023
Roy's Largest Root	0.022	3.207	0.023

Table 11. MANOVA Results Comparing Gender Differences in FLCA of the Second Study

Variable	Male	Female	F	Significance
Communication Apprehension	36.76	35.33	3.769	0.053
Fear of Negative Evaluation	23.99	22.40	9.322	0.002*
General Feeling of Anxiety	37.81	36.11	5.637	0.018*

*Significant at $p < 0.05$.

From Table 11, it can be observed that two variables, namely fear of negative evaluation and general feeling of anxiety, have significant differences between female and male students ($p < 0.05$). Male students experience significantly higher level of anxiety in the categories of fear of negative evaluation and general feeling of anxiety.

The Effect of Gender on FLCA: Discussion of Results from the Two Studies

The descriptive statistical results of the first study indicate that, overall, both males (average FLCA score = 3.29) and females (average FLCA score = 3.16) are fairly anxious in their foreign language classrooms. Further, the independent sample *t*-tests results suggest the male students had significant ($p< 0.05$) higher scores for 13 items on the FLCAS than female students; and ten of them covered all three categories of FLCA (i.e., "communication apprehension," "fear of negative evaluation," and "general feeling of anxiety") and had an average FLCA score of over 3.01 for both genders, indicating that the male students experienced significantly higher levels of FLCA in these areas than the female students. The MANOVA test further confirms that male students experienced significantly higher levels of FLCA in all three categories of "communication apprehension," "fear of negative evaluation," and "general feeling of anxiety" than female students ($p < 0.05$).

The results of the second study were similar in terms of the effect of gender on FLCA; however, students' overall levels of FLCA were lower. The descriptive statistical results indicate that, overall, male students (average FLCA score = 2.99) are slightly anxious in their foreign language classrooms; but female students (average FLCA score = 2.84) are probably not anxious. Further, the independent sample *t*-tests results suggest the male students had significant ($p< 0.05$) higher scores for 9 items on the FLCAS than female students; and only four of them, i.e., 2 (*I don't worry about making mistakes in language class*), 3 (*I tremble when I know that I'm going to be called on in language class*), 10 (*I worry about the consequences of failing my foreign language class*), and 18 (*I feel confident when I speak in foreign language class*) had an average FLCA score of over 3.0 for both genders, indicating that both male and female students lack confidence in speaking the foreign languages and worry about the consequences of failing the language class and are anxious about making mistakes and being called on in the classrooms; however, the male students experienced significantly higher levels of FLCA in these areas than the female students ($p < 0.05$). Finally, the MANOVA test suggests that male students experience significantly higher level of anxiety in the categories of "fear of negative evaluation" and "general feeling of anxiety" ($p < 0.05$), but not in "communication apprehension" category.

The reason for students' overall lower levels of FLCA in the second study than in the first study needs to be further investigated. However, the following may help to explain the difference. Whether learning a foreign language as a major or not makes a difference (Chen and Chang, 2009; Cheng, Horwitz, and Schallert, 1999; Ewald, 2007; Liu and Jackson, 2008; Rodríguez and Abreu, 2003; Yan and Horwitz, 2008; Wu, 2010). Those students who choose to study a foreign language as their major are usually confident in their language skills, spend much effort and time studying it, have more exposure to the foreign language, and tend to use a variety of foreign language-learning strategies more frequently, and therefore, they feel less anxious in the language classroom (Wu, 2010). In the second study, all 436 participants studied English, French, Spanish, German, Japanese, Korean, and Arabic as their majors in the major language university. However, among all the 419 participants learning English as a foreign language at two major comprehensive universities in Beijing, a majority of them (76.4%) were non-English majors, who learn English to meet the program requirements set by the Ministry of Education of China (1999, 2003); only 23.6% of them were English majors. Most of them learn English because

Based on the results of these two studies, a general conclusion about the effect of gender on FLCA would be: Male freshmen students experience significantly higher levels of FLCA than female freshmen students at these Chinese universities. This result is different from what Clarck and Trafford (1996) and Abu-Rabia (2004) had reported, but it is similar to the results as reported by Kitao (2001) and MacIntyre et al. (2002). Further, it confirms Zhao's (2007) result in terms of the effect of gender on the FLCA experienced by Chinese students learning a foreign language. Zhao (2007) examined 115 high school students' FLCA in the context of learning English as a foreign language and reported that male students experience higher levels of FLCA than female students in learning English as a foreign language.

CONCLUSION

This chapter examines the effect of gender on FLCA by briefly reviewing previous FLCA studies and reporting the results of the two empirical studies included in this book. Many empirical studies have been conducted in the area of FLCA and its relation to gender (Abu-Rabia, 2004; Clarck and Trafford, 1995; Dewaele, 2007; Ipek, 2009; Kitano, 200; MacIntyre et al., 2002; Zhao, 2007). Unfortunately, these studies yield conflicting results in terms of the impact of gender on the FLCA experienced by the language learners (Ipek, 2009). The results of the two studies indicate that male freshmen students experience significantly higher levels of FLCA than female freshmen students at three Chinese universities in Beijing. This result confirms Zhao's (2007) result in terms of the effect of gender on the FLCA experienced by Chinese students learning a foreign language. Although many studies will continue to examine this topic and there will also be many discrepant results, it is believed that continuing research in the area of FLCA and gender will provide important implications for both male and female foreign language students as well as classroom teachers.

REFERENCES

Abu-Rabia, S. (2004). Teachers' role, learners' gender differences, and FL anxiety among seventh-grade students studying English as a FL. *Educational Psychology, 24*(5), 711-721.

Chen, I. J., and Chang, C. C. (2009). Cognitive load theory: An empirical study of anxiety and task performance in language learning. *Electronic Journal of Research in Educational Psychology, 7*(2), 729–745.

Cheng, Y. S., Horwitz, E. K., and Schallert, D. L. (1999). Language anxiety: Differentiating writing and speaking components. *Language Learning, 49*(3), 417-446.

Clarck, A., and Trafford, J. (1995). Boys into modern languages: An investigation of the discrepancy in attitudes and performance between boys and girls in modern languages. *Gender and Education, 7*, 315-325.

Dewaele, J. M. (2007). The effect of multilingualism, sociobiographical, and situational factors on communicative anxiety and foreign language anxiety of mature language learners. *International Journal of Bilingualism, 11*(4), 391–409.

Ewald, J. D. (2007). Foreign language learning anxiety in upper-level classes: Involving students as researchers. *Foreign Language Annals, 40*(1), 122–142.

Horwitz, E. K., Horwitz, M. B., and Cope, J. A. (1986). Foreign language classroom anxiety. *The Modern Language Journal, 70*, 125-132.

Horwitz, E. K. (2008). Becoming a language teacher: A practical guide to second language learning and teaching. Boston, MA: Pearson.

Ipek, H. (2009). Foreign language reading anxiety: Proficiency and gender. *The International Journal of Learning, 16*(8), 293-299.

Kitano, K. (2001). Anxiety in the college Japanese language classroom. *The Modern Language Journal, 85*(4), 549-566.

Liu, M. and Jackson, J. (2008). An exploration of Chinese EFL learners' unwillingness to communicate and foreign language anxiety. *The Modern Language Journal, 92*, 71-86.

MacIntyre, P. D., Baker, S. C., Clément, R., and Donovan, L. A. (2002). Sex and age effects on willingness to communicate, anxiety, perceived competence, and L2 motivation among junior high school French immersion students. *Language Learning, 52*(3), 537–564.

Ministry of Education of China. (1999). *Teaching syllabus for college English.* Shanghai: Shanghai Foreign Language Education Press.

Ministry of Education of China. (2003). *English teaching syllabus.* Beijing: People's Press.

Rodríguez, M., and Abreu, O. (2003). The stability of general foreign language classroom anxiety across English and French. *The Modern Language Journal, 87*(3), 365–374.

Wu, K. H. (2010). The relationship between language learners' anxiety and learning strategy in the CLT classrooms. *International Education Studies, 3*(1), 174-191.

Yan, J. X., and Horwitz, E. K. (2008). Learners' perceptions of how anxiety interacts with personal and instructional factors to influence their achievement in English: A qualitative analysis of EFL learners in China. *Language Learning, 58*(1), 151-183.

Zhao, N. (2007). A study of high school students' English learning anxiety. *The Asian EFL Journal, 9*(3), 22-34.

Chapter 5

THE EFFECT OF MAJOR ON FOREIGN LANGUAGE CLASSROOM ANXIETY

ABSTRACT

Whether or not learning a foreign language as a major can have an impact on the foreign language classroom anxiety (FLCA) experienced by its learners (Chen and Chang, 2009; Cheng, Horwitz, and Schallert, 1999; Ewald, 2007; Liu and Jackson, 2008; Rodríguez and Abreu, 2003; Wu, 2010; Yan and Horwitz, 2008) is discussed. For example, foreign language majors have more exposure to the language and are usually confident in their language skills; further, they spend much effort and time studying the language and tend to use a variety of foreign language-learning strategies more frequently. Therefore, they usually feel less anxious in the foreign language classroom than the non-major students (Wu, 2010). This chapter discusses the effect of major on FLCA. It first briefly summarizes the previous literature regarding the effect of major on FLCA. As mentioned in Chapter 3, the first empirical study included in this book examined the effect of major on the FLCA experienced by the Chinese freshmen students at two major universities in Beijing. This chapter briefly describes the research methodology that the first empirical study used to examine the major (English majors vs. non-English majors) effect. Further, it reports the major-related results of the study. Finally, this chapter discusses the results of the study.

BRIEF SUMMARY OF PREVIOUS LITERATURE

Regardless of the conflicting results regarding the effect of major on the FLCA experienced by the language learners, whether or not learning a foreign language as a major has an impact on FLCA (Chen and Chang, 2009; Cheng et al., 1999; Clement, Dornyei, and Noels, 1994; Ewald, 2007; Liu and Jackson, 2008; Rodríguez and Abreu, 2003; Wu, 2010; Yan and Horwitz, 2008). For example, students who study a foreign language as a major usually feel less anxious in the classroom because they are usually confident in their language skills and tend to use a variety of foreign language-learning strategies more frequently (Wu, 2010). However, research also indicates that students who are taking a foreign language class as a major experience higher levels of anxiety because they do not feel confident in their language abilities, and the result of the foreign language class can lead to future career success (Clement et al., 1994; Ewald, 2007). Seven studies are briefly reviewed in the following section; four of them examined the FLCA experienced by majors (Cheng et al., 1999; Ewald, 2007; Rodríguez and Abreu, 2003; Wu, 2010), and three of them investigated the FLCA experienced by non-majors (Chen and Chang, 2009; Liu and Jackson, 2008; Yan and Horwitz, 2008).

The following four studies examined the FLCA experienced by the majors (Cheng et al., 1999; Ewald, 2007; Rodríguez and Abreu, 2003; Wu, 2010). Over a decade ago, Cheng et al. (1999) examined the relationship between FLCA and foreign language writing anxiety as well as their associations with foreign language speaking and writing achievement. The participants were 433 English major students at four universities in Taiwan. A modified Foreign Language Classroom Anxiety Scale (FLCAS) (Horwitz, Horwitz, and Cope, 1986), an adapted second language version of the Daly-Miller Writing Apprehension Test (SLWAT) (Daly, and Miller, 1975), and a background questionnaire were administered to the participants. The results indicate that FLCAS and SLWAT are two related but independent constructs. FLCA is a more general type of anxiety about learning a second language with a strong speaking anxiety element, whereas SLWAT is a language-skill-specific anxiety. However, low self-confidence seems to be an important component of both anxiety constructs, indicating that these Chinese students majoring in English still experience both FLCA and foreign language writing anxiety due to their low self-confidence in their language abilities.

Further, Rodriguez and Abreu (2003) examined the stability of the FLCA construct across English and French languages. The participants were 110 pre-service teachers from two western universities in Venezuela, who were majoring simultaneously in these two foreign languages. Two Spanish versions (one for each language) of the FLCAS (Horwitz et al., 1986) were administered to the participants. The results of the study provided direct evidence suggesting the stability of the construct across both English and French; in other words, these participants majoring in English and French simultaneously experience FLCA.

Recently, through a qualitative analysis of questionnaire data (adapted FLCAS), Ewald (2007) examined the FLCA experienced by 21 students majoring in Spanish at an American university. The results indicate that many of these students experienced FLCA in upper-level classes because many participants did not feel confident in their language abilities. Further, students pointed to the key role of the teacher in producing and relieving FLCA.

Most recently, Wu (2010) examined the relationship between FLCA and learning strategies in the English language classrooms. Sixty-six Chinese adult learners of English (all major students) from a university in Taiwan participated in the study. Results show that the participants experience a high level of anxiety in the English classrooms. They also reported that FLCA has adverse effects on their learning of English. However, the findings reveal that those students who have expended much effort and time studying English tend to use a larger variety of learning strategies more frequently and they feel less anxious when they use English.

In recent years, a few studies investigated the FLCA experienced by non-majors (Chen and Chang, 2009; Liu and Jackson, 2008; Yan and Horwitz, 2008). For example, Liu and Jackson (2008) studied the unwillingness to communicate and FLCA experienced by Chinese learners of English as a foreign language. The participants were 547 first-year non-English majors at a major Chinese university. The participants completed the Unwillingness to Communicate Scale (UCS) (Burgoon, 1976), the Language Class Risk-Taking (LCR) (Ely, 1986) and Language Class Sociability (LCS) (Ely, 1986) scales, and the FLCAS (Horwitz et al., 1986). The results show that most students were willing to participate in interpersonal conversations, but many of them did not like to speak English in class; further, more than onc-third of the students felt anxious in their English classrooms because they feared being negatively evaluated and were apprehensive about public speaking and tests.

Unlike Liu and Jackson (2008), Yan and Horwitz (2008) examined learners' perceptions of how students' anxiety works together with other variables in influencing language learning by using semi-structured interview and grounded-theory analysis. The researchers first administered the FLCAS (Horwitz et al., 1986) to 532 first-year through fourth-year non-English majors in a university in Shanghai, China. Based on their FLCAS scores, participants were classified as having high, moderate, and low levels of anxiety. Twenty-one students with varying levels of anxiety were interviewed for this study. The results show that "comparison with peers," "learning strategies," and "language learning interest and motivation" are the most immediate sources of FLCA in learning English as a foreign language for these Chinese students. Accordingly, Yan and Horwitz (2008) suggested that "helping students develop more effective language-learning strategies, avoid comparisons with other students, and maintain interest and motivation could be useful antidotes" (p. 175) to the reduction of these students' FLCA.

Further, Chen and Chang (2009) examined the relationship among cognitive load, FLCA and task performance. The participants were 88 non-English major students enrolled in a four-year program at a technical university in Taiwan. The FLCAS (Horwitz et al., 1986) was employed to examine their anxiety levels; the Cognitive Load Subject Rating Scale was utilized to measure their cognitive load while engaging in an English listening comprehension task. The results show that students with higher FLCA also incurred a heavier cognitive load and received lower test scores. To enhance learning effectiveness, instructors are encouraged to identify anxiety-provoking situations and provide a supportive learning environment so that the learners can devote their complete working memory resources to the learning tasks.

Although the above studies examined the FLCA experienced by majors or non-majors from multiple perspectives, none of them compared the level or amount of FLCA experienced by both major and non-major students in its design. The first study included in this book, which was designed to investigate the effect of major (English majors vs. non-English majors) on FLCA, could bridge this gap.

Brief Description of Methodology Used to Examine the Effect of Major on FLCA

As mentioned in Chapter 3, the first empirical study included in this book examined the effect of major (English majors vs. non-English majors) on the FLCA experienced by 419 Chinese freshmen students learning English as a foreign language at two major comprehensive universities in Beijing. An expanded FLCAS (Horwitz et al., 1986) (see appendix A) was employed as the survey instrument. The expanded FLCAS included the original 33 items, a demographic information section and three open-ended questions. The expanded FLCAS was first translated into Chinese (see appendix B). The Chinese-language version of the FLCAS was then checked through back-translation, and it was finally pilot tested prior to administration.

In order to examine the effect of major on FLCA, all freshmen students studying English as a foreign language at the two major comprehensive universities in Beijing were invited to participate in the first study. For this study, participants were grouped by major (English majors vs. non-English majors) for data analyses.

Using SPSS, the data obtained for the first study were analyzed at three different levels. Level one analysis involves the descriptive statistics (mean and standard deviation) by major (English majors vs. non-English majors). Level two analysis includes independent sample *t*-tests performed to examine significant major difference in responding to each item on the FLCAS. Level three analysis involves the MANOVAs conducted to examine if there were any significant differences in the three categories of FLCA, namely, communication apprehension, fear of negative evaluation, and general feeling of anxiety experienced by students of different major.

MAJOR-RELATED RESULTS OF THE FIRST STUDY

Major-related results of the first study are reported in the order of descriptive statistical results, independent sample *t*-tests results, and MANOVAs results.

Descriptive Statistical Results

As described in Chapter 3, 419 freshmen students from the two major comprehensive universities in Beijing participated in the first study. Among the 419 participants, 99 (23.6%) were English majors and 320 (76.4%) were non-English majors. The non-English majors were students majoring in mathematics, computer science, engineering, packaging, gardening, and business administration from the two universities. There were approximately three times more non-English major students than English major students.

Table 12 presents a summary of descriptive statistics by major, i.e., the mean and standard deviation for responses to the 33 items on the FLCAS by major. As shown in Table 12, overall, English major students had an average FLCA score of 3.18, and non-English major students had an average FLCA score of 3.25, indicating that both English major and non-English major students are fairly anxious in their English classrooms.

Table 12. Summary of Descriptive Statistics by Major of the First Study

Item	Mean		Std. Deviation	
	English	Non-English	English	Non-English
1	*3.34*	*3.59*	0.98	0.91
2	*3.72*	*4.07*	0.74	0.77
3	*3.44*	*3.63*	0.61	0.67
4	*3.27*	*3.33*	0.51	0.57
5	*3.74*	*3.47*	0.91	0.96
6	2.94	*3.16*	0.86	0.84
7	*3.15*	*3.13*	0.95	0.95
8	*3.10*	*3.02*	0.80	0.81
9	*3.44*	*3.58*	0.56	0.63
10	*3.76*	*3.92*	0.72	0.76
11	*3.08*	2.99	0.79	0.84
12	*3.37*	*3.47*	0.55	0.58
13	2.79	*3.03*	0.82	0.85
14	*3.45*	*3.42*	0.66	0.64
15	2.71	2.78	0.76	0.82
16	2.83	2.86	0.85	0.83
17	2.66	2.78	0.72	0.79
18	*3.32*	*3.19*	0.57	0.47
19	2.47	2.60	0.63	0.72
20	*3.37*	*3.57*	0.56	0.62
21	2.54	2.68	0.61	0.71
22	*3.81*	*3.63*	0.71	0.72
23	2.93	*3.09*	0.91	0.93
24	*3.15*	*3.22*	0.36	0.47
25	2.96	*3.18*	0.86	0.88
26	*3.23*	*3.35*	0.51	0.56
27	*3.20*	*3.27*	0.47	0.52
28	*3.12*	2.97	0.81	0.80
29	*3.18*	*3.30*	0.41	0.55
30	2.93	*3.00*	0.86	0.91
31	*3.15*	*3.23*	0.39	0.49
32	*3.15*	*3.09*	0.87	0.93
33	*3.57*	*3.53*	0.72	0.59
Total	*3.18*	*3.25*	0.24	0.25

However, non-English major students experienced a higher level of FLCA than English major students.

Table 12 also shows that, for English major students, levels of FLCA were found in responses to 23 items except 6, 13, 15, 16, 17, 19, 21, 23, 25 and 30, with items 22 (mean = 3.81), 10 (mean = 3.76), and 5 (mean = 3.74) having the highest means; for non-English major students, levels of FLCA were found in responses to 26 items except 11,15, 16, 17, 19, 21, and 28, with items 2 (mean = 4.07), 10 (mean = 3.92), 3 (mean = 3.63), and 22 (mean = 3.65) having the highest means.

Items 22 (*I don' t feel pressure to prepare very well for language class*) and 10 (*I worry about the consequences of failing my foreign language class*) reflect the first and second highest levels of FLCA for English major students, and the second and third highest levels of FLCA for non-English major students, respectively. However, item 5 (*It wouldn' t bother me at all to take more foreign language classes*) reflects the third highest level of FLCA for English major students; and items 2 (*I don' t worry about making mistakes in language class*) and 3 (*I tremble when I know that I' m going to be called on in language class*) reflect the first and third highest levels of FLCA for non-English major students. As mentioned in Chapters 3 and 4, items 2, 5, and 22 are reverse-scored items on the FLCAS, and students' responses to these items have been switched so that higher scores on these items represent higher levels of FLCA (Horwitz, 2008).

Independent Sample *t*-Tests Results

In addition to descriptive statistical analysis, independent sample *t*-tests were conducted to examine significant major (English majors vs. non-English majors) difference in the FLCA experienced by this group of freshmen students. Table 13 presents the independent sample *t*-tests results.

As shown in Table 13, overall, non-English major students had significantly ($p < 0.001$) higher average scores of the 33 items than English major students, suggesting that non-English majors experienced a significantly higher level of FLCA than English majors. As also shown in Table 13, non-English major students had significantly ($p < 0.05$) higher scores for items 1 (*I never feel quite sure of myself when I am speaking in my foreign language class*), 2 (*I don't worry about making mistakes in language class*), 3 (*I tremble when I know that I'm going to be called on in language class*), 6 (*During language class, I find myself thinking about things that have nothing to do with the course*), 13 (*It embarrasses me to volunteer answers in my language class*), 20 (*I can feel my heart pounding when I'm going to be called on in language class*), and 25 (*Language class moves so quickly I worry about getting left behind*) than English major students, indicating that non-English major students experienced significantly higher levels of FLCA in these areas than English major students. However, English majors had significantly ($p <$ 0.05) higher scores for items 5 (*It wouldn't bother me at all to take more foreign language classes*), 18 (*I feel confident when I speak in foreign language class*), and 22 (*I don't feel pressure to prepare very well for language class*) than non-English majors, indicating that English majors experienced significantly higher levels of FLCA in these areas than non-English majors.

Table 13. Summary of Independent Sample *t*-tests Results by Major of the First Study

Item	Grouping Variable	N	Mean	Std. Deviation	Value of t	Significance
1	English	99	3.34	0.98	-2.327	0.020
	Non-English	320	3.59	0.91		
2	English	99	3.72	0.74	-4.025	0.000
	Non-English	320	4.07	0.77		
3	English	99	3.44	0.61	-2.393	0.017
	Non-English	320	3.63	0.67		
5	English	99	3.74	0.91	2.470	0.014
	Non-English	320	3.47	0.96		
6	English	99	2.94	0.86	-2.261	0.024
	Non-English	320	3.16	0.84		
13	English	99	2.79	0.82	-2.519	0.012
	Non-English	320	3.03	0.85		
18	English	99	3.32	0.57	2.382	0.018
	Non-English	320	3.19	0.47		
20	English	99	3.37	0.56	-2.839	0.005
	Non-English	320	3.57	0.62		
22	English	99	3.81	0.71	2.231	0.026
	Non-English	320	3.63	0.72		
25	English	99	2.96	0.86	-2.202	0.028
	Non-English	320	3.18	0.88		
Total	English	99	3.18	0.24	-2.364	0.019
	Non-English	320	3.25	0.25		

MANOVA Test Results

Finally, MANOVA test was conducted to examine if there were any significant differences in the three categories of FLCA, namely, communication apprehension, fear of negative evaluation, and general feeling of anxiety experienced by students of different majors (English vs. non-English majors). Tables 14 and 15 present the results of the MANOVA test. As shown in Table 14, the four most commonly reported statistical indicators converged to the same equivalent *F*-value. Also, the significant p-value of 0.013 indicates individual between-group differences.

From Table 15, it can be observed that two variables, namely, "communication apprehension" and "fear of negative evaluation" have significant differences between English and non-English major students ($p < 0.05$). Non-English major students experience significantly higher levels of anxiety in the categories of "communication apprehension" and "fear of negative evaluation fear of negative evaluation" than English major students ($p < 0.05$).

Table 14. MANOVA Results Comparing Gender Group on Three Average Summated Scale Scores of the First Study

Test	Value	*F*	Sig.
Pillai's Trace	0.026	3.633	0.013
Wilks' Lambda	0.974	3.633	0.013
Hotelling's Trace	0.026	3.633	0.013
Roy's Largest Root	0.026	3.633	0.013

Table 15. MANOVA Results Comparing Major Differences in FLCA of the First Study

Variable	English	Non-English	*F*	Significance
Communication Apprehension	39.55	40.65	8.025	0.005*
Fear of Negative Evaluation	23.77	24.60	5.822	0.016*
General Feeling of Anxiety	41.58	41.87	0.490	0.484

*Significant at $p < 0.05$.

THE EFFECT OF MAJOR ON FLCA: DISCUSSION OF RESULTS

The descriptive statistical results of this study indicate that, overall, both English majors (average FLCA score = 3.18) and non-English majors (average FLCA score = 3.25) are fairly anxious in their English classrooms. Further, the independent sample *t*-tests results indicate that non-English majors had significantly ($p < 0.001$) higher average scores of the 33 items than English majors, suggesting that non-English majors experienced a significantly higher level of FLCA than English majors. The MANOVA test further indicates non-English major students experience significantly higher levels of anxiety in the categories of "communication apprehension" and "fear of negative evaluation fear of negative evaluation" than English major students ($p < 0.05$).

These significant differences suggest that major as a factor impacts the levels of FLCA experienced by language learners. These results are also consistent with what have been reported in the field (Chen and Chang, 2009; Cheng, Horwitz, and Schallert, 1999; Ewald, 2007; Liu and Jackson, 2008; Rodríguez and Abreu, 2003; Yan and Horwitz, 2008; Wu, 2010). In China, students usually choose to study English as their major after they have started their senior middle school. Students who choose to study English as their major are usually better learners and more confident in their language skills than those who do not choose English as their major. However, those who do not choose English as their major are all required to take English classes for one or two years at universities and colleges and pass the national college English proficiency test(s) (i.e., College English Test Band 3 for three-year college students and College English Test Band 4 for four-year university students) so that they can graduate (Ministry of Education of China, 1999, 2003). These high-stakes tests surely increase their levels of anxiety in the English classrooms.

Similarly, English major students are also required to pass certain tests to meet graduation requirements. However, they take a variety of English classes every year and of course have more exposure to the English language; further, they usually spend much effort and time studying it and tend to use a variety of learning strategies in their study of English. Therefore, they feel less anxious than non-English majors in the English classrooms (Liu and Jackson, 2008; Yan and Horwitz, 2008; Wu, 2010).

Conclusion

Several studies examined the FLCA experienced by major students or non-major students (Chen and Chang, 2009; Cheng, Horwitz, and Schallert, 1999; Ewald, 2007; Liu and Jackson, 2008; Rodríguez and Abreu, 2003; Yan and Horwitz, 2008; Wu, 2010), but none of them compared the level or amount of FLCA experienced by both major and non-major students in its design. This chapter examines the effect of major on FLCA by reporting the results of the first empirical study included in this book, which was designed to investigate the effect of major (English majors vs. non-English majors) on the FLCA experienced by freshmen students as two major universities in China. The results of the first study are consistent with previous research and suggest that major as a factor impacts the levels of FLCA experienced by language learners. The examination of this topic can be a future direction in the field of FLCA research. This topic will have important educational implications for both language students and classroom teachers.

References

Burgoon, J. K. (1976). The unwillingness-to-communicate scale: Development and validation. *Communication Monographs, 43,* 60–69.

Chen, I. J., and Chang, C. C. (2009). Cognitive load theory: An empirical study of anxiety and task performance in language learning. *Electronic Journal of Research in Educational Psychology, 7*(2), 729–745.

Cheng, Y. S., Horwitz, E. K., and Schallert, D. L. (1999). Language anxiety: Differentiating writing and speaking components. *Language Learning, 49*(3), 417-446.

Clément, R., Dörnyei, Z., and Noels, K. A. (1994). Motivation, self-confidence, and group cohesion in the foreign language classroom. *Language Learning, 44*(3), 417–448.

Daly, J. A., and Miller, M. D. (1975). The empirical development of an instrument of writing apprehension. *Research in the Teaching of English, 9*, 242–249.

Ely, C. M. (1986). An analysis of discomfort, risk-taking, sociability, and motivation in the L2 classroom. *Language Learning, 36,* 1–25.

Ewald, J. D. (2007). Foreign language learning anxiety in upper-level classes: Involving students as researchers. *Foreign Language Annals, 40*(1), 122–142.

Horwitz, E. K., Horwitz, M. B., and Cope, J. A. (1986). Foreign language classroom anxiety. *The Modern Language Journal, 70*, 125-132.

Horwitz, E. K. (2008). Becoming a language teacher: A practical guide to second language learning and teaching. Boston, MA: Pearson.

Liu, M. and Jackson, J. (2008). An exploration of Chinese EFL learners' unwillingness to communicate and foreign language anxiety. *The Modern Language Journal, 92*, 71-86.

Ministry of Education of China. (1999). *Teaching syllabus for college English.* Shanghai: Shanghai Foreign Language Education Press.

Ministry of Education of China. (2003). *English teaching syllabus.* Beijing: People's Press.

Rodríguez, M., and Abreu, O. (2003). The stability of general foreign language classroom anxiety across English and French. *The Modern Language Journal, 87*(3), 365–374.

Wu, K. H. (2010). The relationship between language learners' anxiety and learning strategy in the CLT classrooms. *International Education Studies, 3*(1), 174-191.

Yan, J. X., and Horwitz, E. K. (2008). Learners' perceptions of how anxiety interacts with personal and instructional factors to influence their achievement in English: A qualitative analysis of EFL learners in China. *Language Learning, 58*(1), 151-183.

Chapter 6

THE EFFECT OF LANGUAGE ON FOREIGN LANGUAGE CLASSROOM ANXIETY

ABSTRACT

The specific foreign language that learners are learning can have an impact on their foreign language classroom anxiety (FLCA). For example, research shows that non-Western languages such as Japanese, Arabic, Chinese, and Korean are more difficult to learn than Western languages such as English and French; and therefore, can cause higher levels of anxiety (Aida, 1994). This chapter discusses the effect of language on FLCA. It first briefly summarizes the previous literature regarding the effect of language on FLCA. As mentioned in Chapter 3, the second empirical study included in this book examined the effect of language on the FLCA experienced by the Chinese freshmen students at one major language university in Beijing. This chapter then briefly describes the research methodology that the second empirical study used to examine the language (English vs. other Western languages vs. non-Western languages) effect. Further, it reports the language-related results of the study. Finally, this chapter discusses the results of the study.

BRIEF SUMMARY OF PREVIOUS LITERATURE

Current FLCA research examines anxiety issues in a variety of specific foreign language classrooms. The foreign languages involved in the research include both Western (e.g., English and other Western languages such as French, Spanish, and German) and non-Western languages (e.g., Japanese).

Many studies examined FLCA issues in the context of learning English as a foreign language in different countries (e.g., Abu-Rabia, 2004; Chen and Chang, 2009; Chen and Chang, 2004; Cheng, Horwitz, and Schallert, 1999; Duxbury and Tsai, 2010; Gregersen and Horwitz, 2002; Huang, Eslami, and Hu, 2010; Kim, 2009; Liu and Jackson, 2008; Noormohamadi, 2009; Rodríguez and Abreu, 2003; Semmar, 2010; Wu, 2010; Yan and Horwitz, 2008; Zhao, 2007). Several studies investigated FLCA in the context of learning other Western languages, e.g., French, Spanish, and German as foreign languages in the United States (e.g., Allen and Herron, 2003; Casado and Dereshiwsky, 2001; Ewald, 2007; Frantzen and Magnan, 2005; Ganschow and Sparks, 1996; Onwuegbuzie, Bailey, and Daley, 1997; Sparks and Ganschow, 2007; Tallon, 2009; Tittle, 1997; von Wörde, 1998). Further, a few studies included non-Western languages such as Japanese in the examination of FLCA in the United States (e.g., Kitano, 2001; Onwuegbuzie et al., 1997; Saito and Samimy, 1996). This section briefly reviews a selection of six empirical studies in a chronological order, in which both Western and non-Western languages are examined (Chen and Chang, 2004; Kim, 2009; Kitano, 2001; Saito and Samimy, 1996; Tallon, 2009; von Wörde, 1998).

Approximately one and a half decades ago, Saito and Samimy (1996) examined the role of Japanese-as-a-foreign-language classroom anxiety (JFLCA) among other affective variables (i.e., language class risk-taking, language class sociability, strength of motivation, attitude toward the language class, and concern for grade) of students studying Japanese in relation to students' language performance at three different instructional levels (i.e., beginning, intermediate, and advanced). The participants were 257 students enrolled at these three levels of Japanese courses at an American university. A 29-item questionnaire was administered to the participants. The questionnaire, which was comprised of six subscales to measure JFLCA and other affective variables, provided a comprehensive picture of the student's perspectives on studying Japanese. The results indicate that JFLCA was the best predictor for both the intermediate and advanced-level students' performance. Further, the impact of JFLCA becomes more important as Japanese learners' instructional levels increase. Therefore, teachers of Japanese need to "become aware of these differences in terms of the learners' affective states and respond to them accordingly" (p. 247) in order to help learners by reducing the debilitating effect of JFLCA.

Two years later, using both the Foreign Language Classroom Anxiety Scale (FLCAS) (Horwitz, Horwitz, and Cope, 1986) and in-depth interviews, von Wörde (1998) examined the causes of FLCA in French, German, and

Spanish classrooms and the ways to reduce FLCA. The participants were 15 intermediate level students at an American university. The results suggest that FLCA has multiple sources. Some may be associated with the student, the teacher, and the teaching methodology used by the teacher in language classrooms. Further, FLCA may also originate in "low self-esteem, specious beliefs regarding the learning of language, negative experience associated with the foreign language or culture, or the general experience of language learning" (p. 4). It is suggested that the awareness of the problem of the FLCA should be enhanced and taken seriously by both language teachers and students so that an anxiety-free or a low-anxiety classroom environment can be created for foreign language learning.

Similar to the study by Saito and Samimy (1996), Kitano (2001) examined JFLCA in university Japanese classrooms. Specifically, using a shortened FLCAS (Horwitz et al., 1986), Kitano (2001) examined how 212 students' fear of negative evaluation and their self-perceived speaking ability are related to the JFLCA they are experiencing in the Japanese classrooms in two American universities. The results show that there was a positive correlation between students' JFLCA and their fear of negative evaluation but a negative correlation between their JFLCA and their perceived speaking ability. Further, the level of an individual male student's JFLCA was higher as he perceived his speaking ability to be less proficient, whereas for an individual female student, there was no such relationship between her level of JFLCA and her perceived speaking proficiency.

Unlike Saito and Samimy (1996) and Kitano (2001), Chen and Chang (2004) examined English-as-a-foreign-language classroom anxiety (EFLCA) issues. Specifically, they investigated the possible existence of causal links between EFLCA and language-learning difficulties by using the FLCAS (Horwitz et al., 1986) to examine EFLCA and the Foreign Language Screening Instrument for Colleges (FLSI-C) (Ganschow and Sparks, 1991) to explore learning difficulty variables. The subjects were 1,187 students from ten universities and colleges around Taiwan.

Factor analysis, correlation analysis, and stepwise multiple regression analysis of data indicate that English learning difficulties account for 36.80% of variance in EFLCA; further, some anxious students have a history of English learning problems, obtain low grades, suffer difficulties with classroom learning, and exhibit poor developmental skills.

Similarly, Kim (2009) examined EFLCA issues in the context of Korean college students learning English in Korea. Specifically, Kim (2009) examined whether EFLCA and motivational goal orientations remained stable across a reading course and a conversation course. The participants were 59 Korean college students learning English in both courses. The major instruments used in the study were the Korean version of the FLCAS (Horwitz et al., 1986), and the Achievement Motivation Questionnaire (Jung, 1996). In terms of the stability of EFLCA across the two courses, the findings indicate that students' levels of EFLCA vary according to instructional contexts. Further, the students reporting higher levels of EFLCA in the conversation course than in the reading course.

In the same year, Tallon (2009) examined Spanish-as-a-foreign-language classroom anxiety (SFLCA) experienced by 413 university students in the United States. Specifically, Tallon (2009) investigated if heritage students of Spanish experience SFLCA and, if so, what levels of anxiety they experience. A "heritage language student" refers to "a language student who is raised in a home where a non-English language is spoken, who speaks or at least understands the language, and who is to some degree bilingual in that language and in English" (Valdés, 2001, p. 38). The data were collected using the FLCAS (Horwitz et al., 1986). A total of 413 students (209 heritage students and 204 nonheritage students) participated in this study. In general, the mean anxiety scores for the heritage students were lower than the mean anxiety scores for the nonheritage students, although there were a few instances when the heritage students actually had higher anxiety scores. In addition, the heritage students in this study reported lower anxiety scores than other college-level students from previous studies reported in the literature that also used the FLCAS.

Although the above studies examined the FLCA experienced by students learning different languages, none of them compared the level or amount of FLCA experienced by students learning Western languages and those learning non-Western languages in its design. The second study included in this book, which was designed to investigate the effect of language (English vs. other Western languages such as French, German, and Spanish vs. non-Western languages such as Japanese, Korean, and Arabic) on FLCA attempted to bridge this gap.

BRIEF DESCRIPTION OF METHODOLOGY USED TO EXAMINE THE EFFECT OF LANGUAGE ON FLCA

As mentioned in Chapter 3, the second empirical study included in this book examined the effect of language (English vs. other Western languages vs. non-Western languages) on the FLCA experienced by 436 Chinese freshmen students at one major language university in Beijing. An expanded FLCAS (Horwitz et al., 1986) (see appendix A) was employed as the survey instrument. The expanded FLCAS included the original 33 items, a demographic information section and three open-ended questions. The expanded FLCAS was first translated into Chinese (see appendix B). The Chinese-language version of the FLCAS was then checked through back-translation, and it was finally pilot tested prior to administration.

In order to examine the effect of language on FLCA, all freshmen students majoring in English, French, Spanish, Japanese, German, Korean, and Arabic at the major language university in Beijing were invited to participate in the second study. For this study, participants were grouped by language (English vs. other Western languages vs. non-Western languages) for data analyses. Other Western languages include French, Spanish, and German and non-Western languages include Japanese, Korean, and Arabic in the second study.

Using SPSS, the data obtained for the second study were analyzed at three different levels. Level one analysis involves the descriptive statistics (mean and standard deviation) by language (English vs. other Western languages vs. non-Western languages). Level two analysis includes one-way ANOVAs performed to examine significant language differences in responding to each item. If there existed significant differences between language groups, a descriptive *post hoc* analysis was conducted to see where exactly the differences occurred. Level three analysis involves the MANOVA conducted to examine if there were any significant differences in the three categories of FLCA, namely, "communication apprehension," "fear of negative evaluation," and "general feeling of anxiety" experienced by students majoring in different languages.

LANGUAGE-RELATED RESULTS OF THE SECOND STUDY

Language-related results of the second study are reported in the order of descriptive statistical results, one-way ANOVAs results, and MANOVA results.

Descriptive Statistical Results

As described in Chapter 3, four hundred and thirty-six freshmen students from the major language university in Beijing participated in the second study. Among the 436 participants, 171 (39%) were English majors; 111 (26%) were majoring in other Western languages including French, Spanish, and German; and 154 (35%) were majoring in non-Western languages including Japanese, Korean, and Arabic. The participants majoring in English, other Western languages, and non-Western languages were distributed roughly equally.

Table 16 presents a summary of descriptive statistics by language, i.e., the mean and standard deviation for responses to the 33 items and the averages by language groups. As shown in Table 16, overall, the English language group, the other Western languages group, and the non-Western languages group had an average of 2.87, 2.86, and 2.90, respectively, indicating that they are probably not very anxious (Horwitz, 2008).

Table 16 also shows that, for the English language group, levels of anxiety were found in responses to items 2, 3, 4, 7, 9, 10, 11, 15, 18, 20, 23, 24, 29, and 33 (14 items), with items 10 (mean = 3.47), 33 (mean = 3.44), and 2, 4, 20 (mean = 3.29) having the highest means; for the Western language group, levels of anxiety were found in responses to items 2, 3, 4, 7, 8, 9, 10, 11, 12, 18, 20, 23, 25, 28, 29, and 33 (16 items), with items 10 (mean = 3.69), 8 (mean = 3.48), and 33 (mean = 3.34) having the highest means; for the non-Western language group, levels of anxiety were found in responses to items 2, 3, 4, 8, 10, 11, 12, 15, 18, 20, 29, and 33 (12 items), with items 10 (mean = 3.72), 33 (mean = 3.51), and 11 (mean = 3.48) having the highest means.

Item 10 (*I worry about the consequences of failing my foreign language class*) and item 33 (*I get nervous when the language teacher asks questions I haven't prepared in advance*) reflect the highest level of anxiety for all three language groups.

Table 16. Summary of Descriptive Statistics by Language of the Second Study

Item	Mean			Std. Deviation		
	English	Other Western	Non-Western	English	Other Western	Non-Western
1	2.79	2.45	2.52	1.04	0.99	1.01
2	*3.29*	*3.28*	*3.19*	1.21	1.13	1.06
3	*3.16*	*3.19*	*3.09*	1.30	1.14	1.10
4	*3.29*	*3.14*	*3.03*	1.21	1.33	1.17
5	2.65	2.48	2.75	1.19	1.06	1.06
6	2.80	2.59	2.88	1.06	1.05	1.00
7	*3.11*	*3.16*	2.95	1.03	1.07	1.00
8	2.95	*3.48*	*3.27*	1.04	1.00	0.95
9	*3.13*	*3.08*	2.96	1.03	0.98	1.02
10	*3.47*	*3.69*	*3.72*	1.19	1.17	1.00
11	*3.07*	*3.22*	*3.48*	1.09	0.86	0.79
12	2.62	*3.07*	*3.05*	1.03	1.06	0.90
13	2.53	2.52	2.78	1.11	0.93	0.94
14	2.74	2.90	2.88	1.08	1.04	1.02
15	*3.25*	2.84	*3.05*	1.05	1.19	1.19
16	2.50	2.54	2.52	1.08	1.08	0.86
17	2.15	2.02	2.06	1.04	0.98	0.93
18	*3.08*	*3.23*	*3.17*	0.92	0.87	0.83
19	2.16	2.06	2.36	0.91	0.88	0.94
20	*3.29*	*3.24*	*3.16*	1.11	1.06	1.10
21	2.50	2.07	2.42	1.09	0.92	0.95
22	2.80	2.59	2.69	1.00	0.98	0.93
23	*3.15*	*3.22*	2.97	1.18	1.10	1.08
24	*3.13*	2.27	2.52	0.96	0.83	0.89
25	2.54	*3.12*	2.86	1.03	1.14	1.02
26	2.56	2.92	2.72	1.14	1.04	0.94
27	2.59	2.44	2.53	1.02	0.89	0.87
28	2.66	*3.05*	2.99	0.97	0.76	0.85
29	*3.23*	*3.28*	*3.07*	1.10	1.23	1.11
30	2.65	2.54	2.69	0.99	0.83	0.90
31	2.46	2.42	2.59	0.86	0.98	0.99
32	2.88	2.86	2.99	1.00	0.86	0.90
33	*3.44*	*3.34*	*3.51*	0.81	0.87	0.83
Total	2.87	2.86	2.90	0.48	0.47	0.42

However, item 2 (*I don't worry about making mistakes in language class*), item 4 (*It frightens me when I don't understand what the teacher is saying in the foreign language*), and item 20 (*I can feel my heart pounding when I'm going to be called on in language class*) reflect the third highest level of anxiety for the English group; item 8 (*I am usually at ease during tests in my language class*) reflects the second highest level of anxiety for the Western language group; and item 11 (*I don't understand why some people get so upset over foreign language classes*) reflects the third highest levels of anxiety for the non-Western language group.

One-Way ANOVAs Results

In addition to descriptive statistical analysis, one-way ANOVAs were conducted to examine significant language (English vs. other Western languages vs. non-Western languages) difference in the FLCA experienced by this group of freshmen students. Table 17 presents the one-way ANOVAs results.

As shown in Table 17, there were significant ($p < 0.05$) differences between the English language group and the other Western language group for the items 1, 8, 12, 15, 21, 24, 25, 26, and 28 (nine items); between the English language group and the non-Western language group for the items 8, 11, 12, 24, 25, and 28 (six items); between the other Western language group and the non-Western language group for the items 19 and 21 (two items).

Table 17 also shows that the English language group experienced significantly ($p < 0.05$) higher levels of anxiety than the other Western language group for the items 1, 15, 21, and 24 (4 items), and the other Western language group experienced significantly ($p < 0.05$) higher levels of anxiety than the English language group for the items 8, 12, 25, 26, and 28 (five items). The non-Western language group experienced significantly ($p < 0.05$) higher levels of anxiety than the English language group for the items 8, 11, 12, 25, and 28 (five items) and, for item 24, the English language group experienced significantly ($p < 0.05$) higher level of anxiety than the non-Western language group. For the items 19 and 21, the non-Western language group experienced significantly ($p < .05$) higher levels of anxiety than the other Western language group.

Table 17. Summary of One-Way ANOVAs Results by Language of the Second Study

Item	Grouping Variable	N	Mean	Std. Deviation	Value of F	Significance
1	English	171	2.79*	1.04	4.633	0.010
	Other Western	111	2.45*	0.99		
	Non-Western	154	2.52	1.01		
8	English	171	2.95*/#	1.04	10.125	0.000
	Other Western	111	3.48*	1.00		
	Non-Western	154	3.27#	0.95		
11	English	171	3.07*	1.09	7.875	0.000
	Other Western	111	3.22	0.86		
	Non-Western	154	3.48*	0.79		
12	English	171	2.62*/#	1.03	10.088	0.000
	Other Western	111	3.07*	1.06		
	Non-Western	154	3.05#	0.90		
15	English	171	3.25*	1.05	4.513	0.011
	Other Western	111	2.84*	1.19		
	Non-Western	154	3.05	1.19		
19	English	171	2.16	0.91	3.893	0.021
	Other Western	111	2.06*	0.88		
	Non-Western	154	2.36*	0.94		
21	English	171	2.50*	1.09	6.407	0.002
	Other Western	111	2.07*/#	0.92		
	Non-Western	154	2.42#	0.95		
24	English	171	3.13*/#	0.96	34.668	0.000
	Other Western	111	2.27*	0.83		
	Non-Western	154	2.52#	0.89		
25	English	171	2.54*/#	1.03	10.331	0.000
	Other Western	111	3.12*	1.14		
	Non-Western	154	2.86#	1.02		
26	English	171	2.56*	1.14	3.934	0.020
	Other Western	111	2.92*	1.04		
	Non-Western	154	2.72	0.94		
28	English	171	2.66*/#	0.97	8.764	0.000
	Other Western	111	3.05*	0.86		
	Non-Western	154	2.99#	0.85		

MANOVA Test Results

Finally, an MANOVA test was conducted to examine if there were any significant differences in the three categories of FLCA, namely, "communication apprehension," "fear of negative evaluation," and "general feeling of anxiety" experienced by students majoring in different languages (English vs. other Western languages vs. non-Western languages). Tables 18 and 19 present the results of the MANOVA test.

As shown in Table 18, the significant p-value of 0.000 indicates individual between-group differences. From Table 19, it can be observed that the variable of "general feeling of anxiety" has significant ($p < .05$) differences between language groups ($p < 0.05$). The non-Western language group experiences significantly ($p < 0.05$) higher level of FLCA in the category of "general feeling of anxiety" than the English language group.

Table 18. MANOVA Results Comparing Language Groups on Three Average Summated Scale Scores of the Second Study

Test	Value	*F*	Sig.
Pillai's Trace	0.086	6.507	0.000
Wilks' Lambda	0.914	6.640	0.000
Hotelling's Trace	0.094	6.772	0.000
Roy's Largest Root	0.094	13.482	0.000

Table 19. MANOVA Results Comparing Language Differences in FLCA of the Second Study

Variable	English	Other Western	Non-Western	F	Significance
Communication Apprehension	36.41	35.09	35.21	1.988	0.138
Fear of Negative Evaluation	22.85	22.53	22.79	0.176	0.839
General Feeling of Anxiety	35.36*	36.68	37.60*	5.322	0.005*

*Significant at $p < 0.05$.

The Effect of Language on FLCA: Discussion of Results

The descriptive statistical results of this study indicate that, overall, the English language group (average FLCA score = 2.87), the other Western languages group (average FLCA score = 2.86), and the non-Western languages (average FLCA score = 2.90) are probably not very anxious (Horwitz, 2008). However, the one-way ANOVA results indicate significant differences for specific items among these three language groups. For example, the English language group experienced significantly ($p < 0.05$) higher levels of anxiety than the other Western language group for four items (i.e., 1, 15, 21, and 24), whereas the other Western language group experienced significantly ($p < 0.05$) higher levels of anxiety than the English language group for five items (i.e., 8, 12, 25, 26, and 28). Further, the non-Western language group experienced significantly ($p < 0.05$) higher levels of anxiety than the English language group for five items (i.e., 8, 11, 12, 25, and 28). Finally, the MANOVA test indicates significant difference only in one category of FLCA between the non-Western language group and the English language group. Specifically, the non-Western language group experiences significantly ($p < 0.05$) higher level of FLCA in the category of "general feeling of anxiety" than the English language group.

The reason for these students' overall low levels of FLCA in this study needs to be further investigated. However, as discussed in Chapter 5, whether learning a foreign language as a major or not makes a difference (Chen and Chang, 2009; Cheng et al., 1999; Ewald, 2007; Liu and Jackson, 2008; Rodríguez and Abreu, 2003; Yan and Horwitz, 2008; Wu, 2010). All participants in this study were learning these foreign languages as their majors. Foreign language majors are usually confident in their language skills, spend much effort and time studying the foreign language, have more exposure to the language, and tend to use a variety of foreign language-learning strategies more frequently; therefore, they do not feel anxious in the language classroom (Wu, 2010).

However, the significantly higher levels of FLCA experienced by students in the non-Western language group in the category of "general feeling of anxiety" than students in the English language group suggest that language as a factor does impact the levels of FLCA experienced by language learners. Aida (1994) indicated that learning non-Western languages can be more difficult for students than learning Western languages. It "requires approximately 1,320 hours of instruction in an intensive program in languages like Japanese, Arabic, Chinese, and Korean to bring students to the same level of proficiency reached after only 480 hours of instruction in languages like French or Spanish" (p. 155). Thus, students who learn Western languages (e.g., English, French, Spanish, etc.) may experience lower levels of FLCA than those learning the more difficult non-Western languages (e.g., Japanese, Korean, Arabic, etc.).

Conclusion

This chapter examined the effect of language on FLCA by briefly reviewing previous FLCA studies and reporting the results of the second empirical study included in this book. Although many studies examined the FLCA experienced by students learning different languages (e.g., Chen and Chang, 2004; Kim, 2009; Kitano, 2001; Saito and Samimy, 1996; Tallon, 2009; von Wörde, 1998), none of them compared the level or amount of FLCA experienced by students learning Western languages and those learning non-Western languages in its design. The second study included in this book was designed to investigate the effect of language (English vs. other Western languages such as French, German, and Spanish vs. non-Western languages such as Japanese, Korean, and Arabic) on FLCA. The results show that the non-Western language (e.g., Japanese, Korean, and Arabic) students experience significantly ($p < 0.05$) higher level of FLCA in the category of "general feeling of anxiety" than the English language group. It is suggested that future research be conducted to validate these findings.

References

Abu-Rabia, S. (2004). Teachers' role, learners' gender differences, and FL anxiety among seventh-grade students studying English as a FL. *Educational Psychology, 24*(5), 711-721.

Aida, Y. (1994). Examination of Horwitz, Horwitz, and Cope's construct of foreign language anxiety: The case of students of Japanese. *The Modern Language Journal, 78*, 155–168.

Allen, H. W., and Herron, C. (2003). A mixed-methodology investigation of the linguistic and affective outcomes of summer study abroad. *Foreign Language Annals, 36*(3), 370-385.

Casado, M. A., and Dereshiwsky, M. I. (2001). Foreign language anxiety of university students. *College Student Journal, 35*, 539-551.

Chen, I. J., and Chang, C. C. (2009). Cognitive load theory: An empirical study of anxiety and task performance in language learning. *Electronic Journal of Research in Educational Psychology, 7*(2), 729–745.

Chen, T. Y., and Chang, G. B. Y. (2004). The relationship between foreign language anxiety and learning difficulties. *Foreign Language Annals, 37*(2), 279–289.

Cheng, Y. S., Horwitz, E. K., and Schallert, D. L. (1999). Language anxiety: Differentiating writing and speaking components. *Language Learning, 49*(3), 417-446.

Duxbury, J. G. and Tsai, L. L. (2010). The effects of cooperative learning on foreign language anxiety: A comparative study of Taiwanese and American universities. *International Journal of Instruction, 3*(1), 3-18.

Ewald, J. D. (2007). Foreign language learning anxiety in upper-level classes: Involving students as researchers. *Foreign Language Annals, 40*(1), 122–142.

Frantzen, D., and Magnan, S. S. (2005). Anxiety and the true beginner-false beginner dynamic in beginning French and Spanish classes. *Foreign Language Annals, 38*(2), 171–186.

Ganschow, L., and Sparks, R. L. (1991). A screening instrument for the identification of foreign language learning problems. *Foreign Language Annals, 24*, 383-398.

Ganschow, L. and Sparks, R. L. (1996). Anxiety about foreign language learning among high school women. *The Modern Language Journal, 80*, 199-212.

Gregersen, T., and Horwitz, E. K. (2002). Language learning and perfectionism: Anxious and non-anxious language learners' reactions to their own oral performance. *The Modern Language Journal, 86*(4), 562–570.

Horwitz, E. K. (2008). *Becoming a language teacher: A practical guide to second language learning and teaching*. Boston, MA: Pearson.

Horwitz, E. K., Horwitz, M. B., and Cope, J. A. (1986). Foreign language classroom anxiety. *The Modern Language Journal, 70*, 125-132.

Huang, S., Eslami, Z., and Hu, R. J. S. (2010). The relationship between teacher and peer support and English-language learners' anxiety. *English Language Teaching, 3*(1), 32-40.

Jung, Y. (1996). Cultural and contextual influences on goal orientations and the relationships among goal orientations, learning strategies, and achievement: A study of Korean high school students learning English. Unpublished doctoral dissertation, University of Texas, Austin.

Kim, S. Y. (2009). Questioning the stability of foreign language classroom anxiety and motivation across different classroom contexts. *Foreign Language Annals, 42*(1), 138-157.

Kitano, K. (2001). Anxiety in the college Japanese language classroom. *The Modern Language Journal, 85*(4), 549-566.

Liu, M. and Jackson, J. (2008). An exploration of Chinese EFL learners' unwillingness to communicate and foreign language anxiety. *The Modern Language Journal, 92*, 71-86.

Noormohamadi, R. (2009). On the relationship between language learning strategies and foreign language anxiety. *Journal of Pan-Pacific Association of Applied Linguistics, 13*(1), 39-52.

Onwuegbuzie, A. J., Bailey, P., and Daley, C. E. (1997). *Foreign language anxiety among college students.* Paper presented at the Annual Meeting of the Mid-South Educational Research Association, Memphis, TN.

Rodríguez, M., and Abreu, O. (2003). The stability of general foreign language classroom anxiety across English and French. *The Modern Language Journal, 87*(3), 365–374.

Saito, Y., and Samimy, K. K. (1996). Foreign language anxiety and language performance: A study of learner anxiety in beginning, intermediate, and advanced-level college students of Japanese. *Foreign Language Annals, 29*, 239-251.

Semmar, Y. (2010). First-year university students and language anxiety: Insights into the English version of the Foreign Language Classroom Anxiety Scale. *The International Journal of Learning, 17*(1), 81-93.

Sparks, R. L., and Ganschow, L. (2007). Is the Foreign Language Classroom Anxiety Scale measuring anxiety or language skills? *Foreign Language Annals, 40*(2), 260–287.

Tallon, M. (2009). Foreign language anxiety and heritage students of Spanish: A quantitative study. *Foreign Language Annals, 42*(1), 112-137.

Tittle, M. (1997). *The effects of foreign and second language students' irrational beliefs and anxiety on classroom achievement.* Research Report (ERIC Document Reproduction Service No. ED 411 674).

Valdés, G. (2001). Heritage language students: Profiles and possibilities. In J. K. Peyton, D. Randard, and S. McGinnis (Eds.), *Heritage languages in America: Preserving a national resource* (pp. 37–80). Washington, DC: Center for Applied Linguistics.

von Worde, R. (1998). *An investigation of students' perspectives on foreign language anxiety. Unpublished doctoral dissertation.* George Mason University, Fairfax, Virginia.

Wu, K. H. (2010). The relationship between language learners' anxiety and learning strategy in the CLT classrooms. *International Education Studies, 3*(1), 174-191.

Yan, J. X., and Horwitz, E. K. (2008). Learners' perceptions of how anxiety interacts with personal and instructional factors to influence their achievement in English: A qualitative analysis of EFL learners in China. *Language Learning, 58*(1), 151-183.

Zhao, N. (2007). A study of high school students' English learning anxiety. *The Asian EFL Journal, 9*(3), 22-34.

Chapter 7

The Sources of Foreign Language Classroom Anxiety

Abstract

Many studies have shown that foreign language classroom anxiety (FLCA) has multiple sources (Abu-Rabia, 2004; Allen and Herron, 2003; Casado and Dereshiwsky, 2001; Chen and Chang, 2004; Chen and Chang 2009; Ewald, 2007; Kim, 2009; Onwuegbuzie, Bailey, and Daley, 1997; Piniel, 2006; Saito and Samimy, 1996; Semmar, 2010; von Wörde, 1998; Wu, 2010; Yan and Horwitz, 2008; Young, 1990; Zhao, 2007). For example, von Wörde (1998) indicates that some sources may be associated with the student, the teacher, and the teaching methodology used by the teacher in language classrooms. Further, FLCA may also originate in "low self-esteem, specious beliefs regarding the learning of language, negative experience associated with the foreign language or culture, or the general experience of language learning" (p. 4). This chapter discusses the sources of FLCA. It first briefly summarizes the previous literature regarding the sources of FLCA. As mentioned in Chapter 3, both empirical studies included in this book examined the sources of FLCA as reported by the Chinese university freshmen students. This chapter then briefly describes the research methodology that both studies used to examine the sources of FLCA. Further, it reports the research findings of both studies. Finally, this chapter discusses the similarities and differences in reporting sources of FLCA between the two empirical studies.

Brief Summary of Previous Literature

A large number of empirical studies have investigated the sources of FLCA and indicated that FLCA has the following sources: students' fear of speaking and being called on, their fear of negative evaluation, their self-perceived foreign language abilities, their personal learning styles, teachers' classroom teaching methods, competitiveness, unrealistic beliefs, native language problems, and testing (Abu-Rabia, 2004; Allen and Herron, 2003; Casado and Dereshiwsky, 2001; Chen and Chang, 2004; Chen and Chang 2009; Donley 1999; Duxbury and Tsai, 2010; Ewald, 2007; Horwitz , Horwitz, and Cope, 1986; Huang, 1998; Kim, 2009; Kitano, 2001; MacIntyre and Gardner, 1991; Noormohamadi, 2009; Onwuegbuzie et al., 1997; Piniel, 2006; Saito and Samimy, 1996; Semmar, 2010; Tittle, 1997; von Wörde, 1998; Wu, 2010; Xie, Leong, and Feng, 2008; Yan and Horwitz, 2008; Young, 1990, 1991; Zhao, 2007). To categorize these sources, students' personal factors, teacher factors, and cultural factors are the three major categories of sources of FLCA. This section briefly summarizes these three major categories.

First, student personal factors can cause FLCA (Duxbury and Tsai, 2010; Huang, 1998; Zhao, 2007). For example, Zhao (2007) indicated that student personal factors include their low levels of foreign language proficiency, which prevents them from communicating effectively in the language; face-saving characteristics, indicating that they don't like to receive low evaluations or criticism about themselves, and the pressure from the high-stakes foreign language tests and the serious competition among students. Huang (1998) argued that one of the causes for student's learning difficulties and FLCA is the non-automatization of the foreign language used in the classroom. Students usually have to spend time connecting words and translating in their minds, while trying to listen or read at the same time; this would take up a great deal of the working memory volume, reduce attention from listening and reading and therefore create anxiety in students. Further, due to their inadequate foreign language skills, they automatically choose to use their native language in foreign language classrooms. Students' native languages become useful tools that enable them to ask for help, argue a point, and explain an idea. However, in a foreign language classroom, this tool is no longer useful. It decreases their time in practicing the foreign language but increases their anxiety in the classroom (Duxbury and Tsai, 2010).

In addition, the lack of foreign language-learning strategies and limited strategy use in the foreign language classroom can create FLCA in the language learners. Learning strategies, as indicated by Noormohamadi (2009), are the steps a student takes to make learning more effective, efficient, self-directed, and transferable to new situations. Noormohamadi (2009) examined the relationship between FLCA and strategy use and reported that the more anxious students are, the less frequently they use strategies. Noormohamadi (2009) recommended that instructors teach students about different strategies explicitly through modeling how and when to use each strategy.

Second, teacher factors are another major category of sources of the FLCA experienced by the language learners (Ewald, 2007; Piniel, 2006; Young, 1991; Zhao, 2007). Specifically, teachers and the learning environment cause students' anxiety in foreign language classroom. For example, Young (1991) argued that foreign language teachers who believe that their job is to correct students' errors; who feel that they cannot have students working in pairs and small groups because the class may get out of control; who believe that the language teacher should do most of the talking and teaching; and who think their role is "more like a drill sergeant's than a facilitator's" (p. 428) may be contributing to students' FLCA. Further, Ewald (2007) claimed that language students tend to feel anxiety when called on randomly in foreign language classes, during language tests and error correction by the teacher in the classroom. Interestingly, Zhao (2007) reported that the lack of native-speaking teachers and over-emphasis of reading and writing in the classroom by the teachers cause students' FLCA.

Finally, cultural factors are also contributing to language learners' FLCA (Wu, 2010; Zhao, 2007). For example, some foreign language learners can be uncommunicative and passive in the learning process. One contributing factor, especially in students from Asian countries, is traditional culture. "Confucian influences are regarded as the main cause of perceived reticence in students from Asian countries" (Wu, 2010, p. 176). In these countries, as Wu (2010) commented, students often have a lack of experience in speaking English, the teacher dominates the learning process, self-expression is often discouraged, the demonstration of knowledge rather than the transformation is valued, and there are high performance expectations. Zhao (2007) further confirmed that, in most Chinese English-as-a-foreign-language (EFL) classrooms, teachers play the role of controller or dominator. Students often feel nervous or oppressed in the EFL classrooms. Consequently, they are not provided a free, relaxed environment for English learning. Finally, Zhao (2007) indicated that the high expectations of Chinese parents for their children can be an important cultural factor. Such high expectations usually do not encourage students, but often result in more anxiety.

Brief Description of Methodology Two Studies Used to Examine the Sources of FLCA

As mentioned in Chapter 3, both empirical studies included in this book examined students' perspectives of the sources of FLCA. The first study involved 419 Chinese freshmen students at two major comprehensive universities in Beijing. The second study involved 436 Chinese freshmen students at one major language university in Beijing.

An expanded FLCAS (Horwitz et al., 1986) (see appendix A) was employed as the survey instrument. The expanded FLCAS included the original 33 items, a demographic information section and three open-ended questions. The expanded FLCAS was first translated into Chinese (see appendix B). The Chinese-language version of the FLCAS was then checked through back-translation, and it was finally pilot tested prior to administration.

The first open-ended question asked about participants' perspectives of the major sources of their FLCA. The data obtained from the participants' responses to the first open-ended question were analyzed identically for both studies. Specifically, their responses to the first open-ended question were sorted and categorized, and major recurring themes were identified and analyzed, with each theme representing a major source of their reported FLCA.

Five Major Sources of FLCA Reported by the First Study

As mentioned above, 419 freshmen students from two major comprehensive universities in Beijing participated in the first study. Among the 419 participants, 99 (23.6%) were English majors and 320 (76.4%) were non-English majors; 221 (52.7%) were male and 198 (47.3%) were female students. The first open-ended question on the expanded FLCAS asked the participants why they feel anxious in the foreign language classroom. Of the 419 participants, 338 (81.5%) answered this question and made a total of 751 individual responses. These 751 individual responses were further sorted into different categories, with each category representing a major source of FLCA.

The following five major sources of FLCA were reported by the first study: a) insufficient English skills, b) personal issues, c) lack of effective learning strategies, d) teacher factors, and e) grading/testing concerns. Table 20 presents a summary of these sources. It shows the total number and percentage of responses that fits into each category, sorted by gender (male vs. female) as well as by major (English vs. non-English).

As shown in Table 20, the reported five major sources of FLCA, which were ranked from the most responses to the least, are: a) insufficient English skills (43.4%), b) personal issues (23.2%), c) lack of effective learning strategies (14.8%), d) teacher factors (12%), and e) grading/testing concerns (6.7%). Both gender (male vs. female) and major (English vs. non-English) groups ranked the sources of FLCA in the same order, with the exception of the English majors, who ranked "lack of effective learning strategies" (19.5%) as the second major source and "personal responses" (17.5%) as the third. Having "insufficient English skills" was consistently ranked as the largest source of FLCA across both gender and major groups, while having "grading/testing concerns" was repeatedly ranked as the smallest.

Table 20. Major Sources of FLCA from the First Study: Total Number and Percentage of Responses

	Gender		Major		
Source	Male	Female	English	Non-English	Total
Insufficient English skills	164 (45.3%)	162 (41.6%)	89 (44.5%)	237 (43%)	326 (43.4%)
Personal issues	85 (23.5%)	89 (22.9%)	35 (17.5%)	139 (25.2%)	174 (23.2%)
Lack of effective learning strategies	46 (12.7%)	65 (16.7%)	39 (19.5%)	72 (13.1%)	111 (14.8%)
Teacher factors	45 (12.4%)	45 (11.6%)	23 (11.5%)	67 (12.2%)	90 (12%)
Grading/testing concerns	22 (6.1%)	28 (7.2%)	14 (7%)	36 (6.5%)	50 (6.7%)
Subtotal	362 (100%)	389 (100%)	200 (100%)	551 (100%)	751 (100%)
Total Responses	751		751		751

Insufficient English Skills

English skills are important for Chinese students in their English classrooms. Students having poor English skills have challenges in understanding class lectures and discussions. Insufficient English skills become the largest source of their FLCA. As shown in Table 20, a total of 326 individual responses were under the category of "insufficient English skills." Male (with 164 responses) and female (with 162 responses) participants made approximately the same number of responses, which mirrored the similar number of participants across the gender group, i.e., among 419 participants, 221 (52.7%) were male and 198 (47.3%) female students. However, due to the different number of participants, i.e., among 419 participants, 99 (23.6%) were English majors and 320 (76.4%) non-English majors, English majors (with 89 responses) made one-and-a-half times fewer responses than non-English majors (with 237 responses). These results suggest that both gender and major groups of participants agreed that their insufficient English skills became the largest source of their FLCA. Insufficient English skills, as reflected in their responses, indicate insufficient listening, speaking, reading, and writing skills in English as well as limited English pronunciation, grammar, and vocabulary. Sample responses under this category include "not good at English," "poor oral English," "small vocabulary," and "afraid of making mistakes due to poor listening and speaking skills."

Personal Issues

Personal issues become the second-largest source of their FLCA. As shown in Table 20, a total of 174 individual responses were under the category of "personal issues." Male (with 85 responses) and female (with 89 responses) participants made approximately the same number of responses, which mirrored the similar number of participants across the gender group, i.e., among 419 participants, 221 (52.7%) were male and 198 (47.3%) female students. However, due to the different number of participants, i.e., among 419 participants, 99 (23.6%) were English majors and 320 (76.4%) non-English majors, English majors (with 35 responses) made three times fewer responses than non-English majors (with 139 responses). These results suggest that both gender and major groups of participants agreed that personal issues became the second-largest source of their FLCA. Personal issues, as reflected in their responses, indicate insufficient learning motivation and interest, lack of self-confidence, and shyness. Sample responses under this category include "having little interest in English," "having no confidence," "afraid of losing face," "afraid of being asked to answer questions," and "afraid of speaking in front of others."

Lack of Effective Learning Strategies

Effective learning strategies are important for Chinese students in their English classrooms. Students with poor learning strategies face considerable challenges in foreign language learning. Lack of effective learning strategies become the third-largest source of their FLCA. As shown in Table 20, a total of 111 individual responses were under the category of "lack of effective learning strategies." Female (with 65 responses) participants made approximately one-third more responses than male (with 46 responses) participants. Despite the fact that there were approximately three times more non-English major participants than English major participants, non-English majors (with 72 responses) made twice as many responses as English majors (with 39 responses). Although a slightly different number of responses was made across gender and major groups of participants, these results still indicate that lack of effective learning strategies contributes largely to their FLCA. Lack of effective learning strategies, as reflected in their responses; indicate insufficient class preparation, poor questioning skills, and inability of getting the main idea. Sample responses under this category include "not well prepared," "not knowing how to ask questions in class," and "not being able to get the main idea of what the teacher has taught."

Teacher Factors

Teachers play an important role in foreign language classrooms. Those with effective language teaching methods facilitate students' foreign language learning in the classroom. Factors associated with teachers are reported as the fourth-largest source of FLCA by the participants. As shown in Table 20, a total of 90 individual responses were under the category of "teacher factors." Male (with 45 responses) and female (with 45 responses) participants made exactly the same number of responses. Non-English majors (with 67 responses) made approximately two times more responses than English majors (with 23 responses) because there were more non-English majors than

English-majors who participated in the study. These results indicate little difference across gender and major groups. Teacher factors, as reflected in their responses, indicate teachers' fast speaking rate, their strictness with students, and their poor teaching methods. Sample responses under this category include "teacher speaking too fast," "hard to understand the teacher," "teacher being too strict with us," and "teacher not offering clear and easy-to-understand explanations and clarifications."

Grading/Testing Concerns

Test anxiety negatively affects students' learning of a foreign language. It also causes students' FLCA. Being anxious about testing and getting a poor grade becomes the fifth-largest source of their FLCA. As shown in Table 20, a total of 50 individual responses were under the category of "grading/testing concerns." Male (with 22 responses) and female (with 28 responses) participants made approximately the same number of responses. Non-English majors (with 36 responses) made more than two times the responses than English majors (with 14 responses) because there were more non-English majors than English-majors who participated in the study. Again, these results did not indicate large difference across both gender and major groups. Grading/testing concerns, as reflected in their responses, indicate their anxiety in taking a test, their fear of being evaluated negatively, as well as their being afraid of receiving a poor course grade. Sample responses under this category include "anxious about taking a test," "scared about receiving negative feedback," "afraid of being graded on what I say wrong," and "afraid of getting a low course mark."

Six Major Sources of FLCA Reported by the Second Study

Four hundred and thirty-six freshmen students participated in the second study. Among the 436 participants, 171 (39%) were English majors, 111 (26%) majoring in other Western languages including French, Spanish, and German, and 154 (35%) majoring in non-Western languages including Japanese, Korean, and Arabic. Of the 436 participants, 97 (22%) were male and 339 (78%) were female students. Like the first empirical study, the participants of the second study were asked to complete the expanded FLCAS. The first open-ended question on the expanded FLCAS asked the participants why they feel anxious inside the foreign language classroom setting by identifying top-three causes. Of the 436 participants, 336 (77.1%) answered this question and identified a total of 803 individual sources. These 803 individual sources were further sorted into different categories, with each category representing a major source of FLCA.

Table 21. Major Sources of FLCA from the Second Study: Total Number and Percentage of Responses

Source	Gender		Language			Total
	Male	Female	English	Other Western	Non-Western	
Insufficient foreign language skills	48 (33.8%)	210 (31.8%)	121 (30.2%)	78 (33.8%)	59 (34.5%)	258 (32.1%)
Personal issues	35 (24.6%)	178 (26.9%)	111 (27.7%)	64 (27.7%)	38 (22.2%)	213 (26.5%)
Lack of effective learning strategies	23 (16.2%)	104 (15.7%)	56 (14%)	36 (15.6%)	35 (20.5%)	127 (15.8%)
Teacher factors	18 (12.7%)	92 (13.9%)	46 (11.5%)	41 (17.7%)	23 (13.5%)	110 (13.7%)
Difficulty of the foreign language	10 (7%)	42 (6.4%)	35 (8.7%)	7 (3%)	10 (5.8%)	52 (6.5%)
Poor attitude toward learning	8 (5.6%)	35 (5.3%)	32 (8%)	5 (2.2%)	6 (3.5%)	43 (5.4%)
Subtotal	142 (100%)	661 (100%)	401 (100%)	231 (100%)	171 (100%)	803 (100%)
Total Responses	803		803			803

The following six major sources of FLCA were reported from the second study: a) insufficient foreign language skills, b) personal issues, c) lack of effective learning strategies, d) teacher factors, e) difficulty of the foreign language, and f) poor attitude toward learning. Table 21 presents a summary of these sources. It shows the total number and percentage of responses that fits into each category, sorted by gender (male vs. female) as well as by language (English vs. other Western languages vs. non-Western languages).

As shown in Table 21, the reported six major sources of FLCA, which were ranked from the most responses to the least, are: a) insufficient foreign language skills (32.1%), b) personal issues (26.5%), c) lack of effective learning strategies (15.8%), d) teacher factors (13.7%), e) difficulty in the foreign language (6.5%), and f) poor attitude toward learning (5.4%). Both gender (male vs. female) and language (English vs. other Western languages vs. non-Western languages) groups ranked the sources of FLCA in the same order, with the exception of the other Western languages group of participants, who ranked "teacher factors" (17.7%) as the third major source and "lack of effective learning strategies" (15.6%) as the fourth. Having "insufficient foreign language skills" was consistently ranked as the largest source of FLCA across both gender and language groups, while having "poor attitude toward learning" was repeatedly ranked as the smallest.

Insufficient Foreign Language Skills

Insufficient foreign language skills become the largest source of Chinese freshmen students' FLCA. As shown in Table 21, a total of 258 individual responses were under the category of "insufficient foreign language skills." Due to the different number of participants, i.e., among 436 participants, 97 (22%) were male and 339 (78%) were female participants, male participants (with 48 responses) made three times fewer responses than female participants (with 210 responses). Obviously, English major participants (with 121 responses) made far more responses than those participants majoring in other Western languages (with 78 responses) and non-Western languages (59 responses), which might be due to different number of participants across the language group, i.e., among the 436 participants, 171 (39%) were English majors; 111 (26%) were majoring in other Western languages; and 154 (35%) were majoring in non-Western languages. These results suggest that both gender and language groups of participants agreed that their insufficient foreign language skills became the largest source of their FLCA. Insufficient foreign language skills, as reflected in their responses, indicate insufficient listening, speaking, reading, and writing skills in the foreign language as well as limited pronunciation, grammar, and vocabulary in the foreign language.

Sample responses under this category include "not good at the foreign language," "poor listening and speaking skills," "small vocabulary," and "afraid of making mistakes due to poor foreign language skills."

Personal Issues

Personal issues become the second-largest source of Chinese freshmen students' FLCA. As shown in Table 21, a total of 213 individual responses were under the category of "personal issues." Due to the fact that there were much fewer male participants than female participants, male participants (with 35 responses) made over three times fewer responses than female participants (with 178 responses). Since English major participants (with 111 responses) are the largest single-language group, they made far more responses than those participants majoring in other Western languages (with 64 responses) and non-Western languages (38 responses). These results indicate little difference across both gender and language groups of participants. Personal issues, as reflected in their responses, indicate insufficient learning motivation and interest, lack of confidence, and shyness. Sample responses under this category include "having little interest in the foreign language," "having no confidence at all," "afraid of making mistakes and losing face," "afraid of being asked to answer questions in the foreign language," and "afraid of speaking the foreign language in front of others."

Lack of Effective Learning Strategies

Lack of effective learning strategies become the third-largest source of Chinese freshmen students' FLCA. As shown in Table 21, a total of 127 individual responses were under the category of "lack of effective learning strategies." Due to the fact that there were much fewer male participants than female participants, male participants (with 23 responses) made approximately four times fewer responses than female participants (with 104 responses). Since English major participants (with 56 responses) are the largest single-language group, they made far more responses than those participants majoring in other Western languages (with 36 responses) and non-Western languages (35 responses). These results indicate little difference across both gender and language groups of participants. Lack of effective learning strategies, as reflected in their responses; indicate insufficient class preparation, poor questioning skills, and inability to get the important information. Sample responses under this category include "not well prepared," "not knowing how to ask questions in the foreign language," and "not being able to understand what is important and what is not important in class."

Teacher Factors

Teacher factors become the fourth-largest source of Chinese freshmen students' FLCA. As shown in Table 21, a total of 110 individual responses were under the category of "teacher factors." Due to the fact that there were much fewer male participants than female participants, male participants (with 18 responses) made approximately four times fewer responses than female participants (with 92 responses). Although English major participants (with 46 responses) are the largest single-language group, they made approximately similar number of responses as those participants majoring in other Western languages (with 41 responses), but twice as many responses as those participants majoring in non-Western languages (23 responses). These results indicate little difference across gender group but large deference between participants majoring in non-Western languages and those majoring in English and other Western languages. Teacher factors, as reflected in their responses, indicate teachers' high speaking rate, their strictness with students, and their problematic teaching methods. Sample responses under this category include "teacher speaking too fast in class," "hard to understand the teacher," "teacher being too strict with us," and "teacher not offering clear explanations and clarifications."

Difficulty of the Foreign Language

Difficulty of the foreign language becomes the fifth-largest source of Chinese freshmen students' FLCA. As shown in Table 21, a total of 52 individual responses were under the category of "difficulty of the foreign language." Again, because there were much fewer male participants than female participants, male participants (with ten responses) made approximately three times fewer responses than female participants (with 42 responses). Since English major participants (with 35 responses) are the largest single-language group, they made far more responses than those participants majoring in other Western languages (with seven responses) and non-Western languages (ten responses). These results indicate little difference across both gender and language groups of participants. Difficulty of the foreign language, as reflected in their responses, indicate the difficulty and complexity of the foreign language they are learning. More specifically, the participants reported their challenges in listening, speaking, reading, writing, pronunciation, vocabulary, and grammar in the foreign language. Sample responses under this category include "The language is simply too hard," "It's hard to use the language," and "The pronunciation and grammar are too complicated."

Poor Attitude toward Learning

The participants reported that they became anxious in the foreign language classroom because they had poor attitude toward learning. As shown in Table 21, a total of 43 individual responses were under the category of having "poor attitude toward learning." Again, since there were much fewer male participants than female participants, male participants (with eight responses) made approximately three times fewer responses than female participants (with 35 responses). However, English major participants (with 32 responses) made over five times more responses than those participants majoring in other Western languages (with five responses) and non-Western languages (six responses). These results indicate little difference across gender group but large difference between participants majoring in English and those majoring in other Western languages and non-Western languages. Poor attitude toward learning, as reflected in their responses, indicate participants' absent-mindedness and irresponsibility in learning the foreign language. Sample responses under this category include "I easily get absent-minded in the foreign language classroom," and "I often do not finish course assignments."

Similarities and Differences between the Two Studies

As shown in Table 22, there were two major similarities and two major differences in reporting sources of FLCA between the two empirical studies.

First, both studies reported the following four identical major sources of FLCA: a) insufficient foreign language skills, b) personal issues, c) lack of effective learning strategies, and d) factors associated with foreign language teachers.

Second, despite the fact that there were similar number of male and female participants in the first study and there were three times more female than male participants in the second study, both studies found little gender difference in terms of total number of responses for each source of FLCA.

Table 22. Similarities and Differences in Reporting Sources of FLCA between the Two Studies

Similarities	Differences
1. Both studies reported the identical four-largest sources of FLCA.	1. The first study found a different fifth-largest source of FLCA from the second study, whereas the second study found two additional major sources of FLCA.
2. Both studies found little gender difference in terms of total number of responses for each source of FLCA.	2. The first study found little difference between English and non-English majors in terms of the total number responses for each source of FLCA. However, the second study found large difference between participants majoring in different foreign languages for certain sources of FLCA.

Third, in the first study, having "grading/testing concerns" became the fifth-largest source of FLCA, whereas in the second study, "difficulty of the foreign language" and "poor attitude toward learning" became the fifth- and sixth-largest sources of FLCA, respectively.

Finally, the first study found little difference between English and non-English majors in terms of the total number responses for each source of FLCA. However, the second study found a large difference between participants majoring in English and other Western languages and those majoring in non-Western languages for the fourth-largest source of FLCA (i.e., teacher factors), and also between participants majoring in English and those majoring in other Western languages and non-Western languages for the sixth-largest source of FLCA (i.e., poor attitude toward learning).

Conclusion

This chapter discussed the sources of FLCA. It first briefly summarized the previous literature regarding the different sources of FLCA. As described in the literature (Abu-Rabia, 2004; Allen and Herron, 2003; Casado and Dereshiwsky, 2001; Chen and Chang, 2004; Chen and Chang 2009; Donley 1999; Duxbury and Tsai, 2010; Ewald, 2007; Horwitz , Horwitz, and Cope, 1986; Huang, 1998; Kim, 2009; Kitano, 2001; MacIntyre and Gardner, 1991; Noormohamadi, 2009; Onwuegbuzie et al., 1997; Piniel, 2006; Saito and Samimy, 1996; Semmar, 2010; Tittle, 1997; von Wörde, 1998; Wu, 2010; Xie, Leong, and Feng, 2008; Yan and Horwitz, 2008; Young, 1990, 1991; Zhao, 2007), FLCA can be caused by students' personal factors, teacher factors, and cultural factors. The results of the two empirical studies included in this book confirmed the findings from previous studies. To examine the sources of FLCA is the first step; the next one is to find ways to alleviate FLCA.

References

Abu-Rabia, S. (2004). Teachers' role, learners' gender differences, and FL anxiety among seventh-grade students studying English as a FL. *Educational Psychology, 24*(5), 711-721.

Allen, H. W., and Herron, C. (2003). A mixed-methodology investigation of the linguistic and affective outcomes of summer study abroad. *Foreign Language Annals, 36*(3), 370-385.

Casado, M. A., and Dereshiwsky, M. I. (2001). Foreign language anxiety of university students. *College Student Journal, 35*, 539-551.

Chen, I. J., and Chang, C. C. (2009). Cognitive load theory: An empirical study of anxiety and task performance in language learning. *Electronic Journal of Research in Educational Psychology, 7*(2), 729–745.

Chen, T. Y., and Chang, G. B. Y. (2004). The relationship between foreign language anxiety and learning difficulties. *Foreign Language Annals, 37*(2), 279–289.

Donley, P. M. (1999). Language anxiety and how to manage it: What educators need to know. *Mosaic, 6*(3), 3-9.

Duxbury, J. G. and Tsai, L. L. (2010). The effects of cooperative learning on foreign language anxiety: A comparative study of Taiwanese and American universities. *International Journal of Instruction, 3*(1), 3-18.

Ewald, J. D. (2007). Foreign language learning anxiety in upper-level classes: Involving students as researchers. *Foreign Language Annals, 40*(1), 122–142.

Horwitz, E. K., Horwitz, M. B., and Cope, J. A. (1986). Foreign language classroom anxiety. *The Modern Language Journal, 70*, 125-132.

Huang, J. F. (1998). *Students' learning difficulties in a second language speaking classroom.* Paper presented at the Annual Meeting of the American Educational Research Association, San Diego, CA. (ERIC Document Reproduction Service No. ED 420 193).

Kim, S. Y. (2009). Questioning the stability of foreign language classroom anxiety and motivation across different classroom contexts. *Foreign Language Annals, 42*(1), 138-157.

Kitano, K. (2001). Anxiety in the college Japanese language classroom. *The Modern Language Journal, 85*(4), 549-566.

MacIntyre, P. D. and Gardner, R. C. (1991). Methods and results in the study of anxiety and language learning: A review of the literature. *Language Learning, 41*(1), 85-117.

Noormohamadi, R. (2009). On the relationship between language learning strategies and foreign language anxiety. *Journal of Pan-Pacific Association of Applied Linguistics, 13*(1), 39-52.

Onwuegbuzie, A. J., Bailey, P., and Daley, C. E. (1997). *Foreign language anxiety among college students.* Paper presented at the Annual Meeting of the Mid-South Educational Research Association, Memphis, TN.

Piniel, K. (2006). Foreign language classroom anxiety: A classroom perspective. In M. Nikolov and J. Horváth (Eds.), *UPRT 2006: Empirical studies in English applied linguistics* (pp. 39-58). Pécs: Lingua Franca Csoport.

Saito, Y., and Samimy, K. K. (1996). Foreign language anxiety and language performance: A study of learner anxiety in beginning, intermediate, and advanced-level college students of Japanese. *Foreign Language Annals, 29*, 239-251.

Semmar, Y. (2010). First-year university students and language anxiety: Insights into the English version of the Foreign Language Classroom Anxiety Scale. *The International Journal of Learning, 17*(1), 81-93.

Tittle, M. (1997). *The effects of foreign and second language students' irrational beliefs and anxiety on classroom achievement*. Research Report (ERIC Document Reproduction Service No. ED 411 674).

von Worde, R. (1998). *An investigation of students' perspectives on foreign language anxiety. Unpublished doctoral dissertation*. George Mason University, Fairfax, Virginia.

Wu, K. H. (2010). The relationship between language learners' anxiety and learning strategy in the CLT classrooms. *International Education Studies, 3*(1), 174-191.

Xie, D., Leong, F. T. L., and Feng, S. (2008). Culture-specific personality correlates of anxiety among Chinese and Caucasian students. *Asian Journal of Social Psychology, 11*, 163-174.

Yan, J. X., and Horwitz, E. K. (2008). Learners' perceptions of how anxiety interacts with personal and instructional factors to influence their achievement in English: A qualitative analysis of EFL learners in China. *Language Learning, 58*(1), 151-183.

Young, D. J. (1990). An investigation of students' perspectives on anxiety and speaking. *Foreign Language Annals, 23*(6), 539-553.

Young, D. J. (1991). Creating a low-anxiety classroom environment: What does language anxiety research suggest? *The Modern Language Journal, 75*, 426-439.

Zhao, N. (2007). A study of high school students' English learning anxiety. *The Asian EFL Journal, 9*(3), 22-34.

Chapter 8

STUDENTS' RESPONSIBILITIES FOR REDUCING THEIR OWN FOREIGN LANGUAGE CLASSROOM ANXIETY

ABSTRACT

Students should take responsibility for their own foreign language learning (Rubin and Thompson, 1982). They have certain responsibilities for reducing their foreign language classroom anxiety (FLCA) (Cauce, Felner, and Primavera, 1982; Crookall and Oxford, 1991; Dewaele, Petrides, and Furnham, 2008; Donley, 1996; Foss and Reitzel, 1988; Hartup, 1989; Huang, Eslami, and Hu, 2010; Nakatani, 2010; Noormohamadi, 2009; Semmar, 2010; von Wörde, 1998; Wentzel, 1994; Young, 1991). For example, they should be aware of the types of anxiety they face in the foreign language classrooms and try to reduce their FLCA in order to manage and take control of their foreign language learning. Further, they should become familiar with their own language-learning styles and develop effective strategies to reduce their FLCA (Semmar, 2010). This chapter discusses students' responsibilities for reducing their FLCA. It first briefly summarizes the previous literature. As mentioned in Chapter 3, both empirical studies included in this book examined students' responsibilities for reducing their own FLCA as reported by the Chinese university freshmen students. This chapter then briefly describes the research methodology that both studies used to examine students' responsibilities. Further, it reports the research findings of both studies. Finally, this chapter discusses the similarities and differences in reporting students' responsibilities for reducing FLCA between the two empirical studies.

BRIEF SUMMARY OF PREVIOUS LITERATURE

Successful foreign language learners should take the responsibility for their own language learning (Rubin and Thompson, 1982). Further, many studies have examined students' responsibilities for reducing their own FLCA (Cauce et al., 1982; Crookall and Oxford, 1991; Dewaele et al., 2008; Donley, 1996; Foss and Reitzel, 1988; Hartup, 1989; Huang et al., 2010; Nakatani, 2010; Noormohamadi, 2009; Semmar, 2010; von Wörde, 1998; Wentzel, 1994; Young, 1991). This section briefly summarizes these responsibilities.

First, language learners should be responsible for their own foreign language learning. Rubin and Thompson (1982) attempted to examine the characteristics of good language learners and reported that good language learners should have the "ability to find their own way, take charge of their learning, organize information about language, and make opportunities for practice in using the language inside and outside the classroom" (as cited in Semmar, 2010, p. 81). Further, language learners should be aware of the types of anxiety they face in the foreign language classrooms and try to reduce their FLCA in order to manage and take control of their foreign language learning (Semmar, 2010).

Second, language learners should become familiar with their own language-learning styles and develop strategies that reduce their anxiety and facilitate their foreign language learning in the classroom (Crookall and Oxford, 1991; Donely, 1996; Foss and Reitzel, 1988; Nakatani, 2010; Noormohamadi, 2009; Semmar, 2010). Foss and Reitzel (1988) suggested that anxious students practice in a small group before they speak in front of the whole class. They also suggested that they create a list of fears or beliefs about speaking in a new language and share with other students who may be feeling the same way. They can understand that their initial fear is normal.

Further, Crookall and Oxford (1991) suggested that anxious students write a letter to an "agony column" (p. 145) explaining some challenges in learning a foreign language and asking for advice. The students can then work together to find ways to overcome these challenges. In addition, Crookall and Oxford (1991) mentioned that the "mistakes panel" (p. 147) might be a good activity that makes anxious students more relaxed and less anxious about making mistakes. Specifically, "students collect mistakes and errors, treating such in a fun manner by awarding points for the most entertaining or original mistakes" (cited in von, 1998, p. 50). They create a positive and collaborative learning environment in the classroom by sharing with the teacher and other students; at the same time, their FLCA is reduced and, ultimately, they can learn from their mistakes.

Furthermore, Young (1991) advised that anxious students should actively seek help in order to manage their FLCA. They can join language clubs, form support groups, and keep a journal as a way to record their feelings and emotions. By keeping a journal, as Young (1991) argued, students can recognize their feelings of inadequacy, and they may arrive at more realistic expectations.

Similar to what previous researchers have suggested, Donely (1996) recommended the following strategies for students to help reduce their anxiety in foreign language classrooms. For example, anxious students should discuss their feelings with the teacher; tell the teacher how they feel; attend every class and be prepared; do something fun and relaxing; eat healthy and get enough sleep and exercise; keep their foreign language class in perspective; seek out opportunities to practice the language; remember that errors are a part of learning; and develop their own standards for rewards and success.

Third, collaborative learning and peer support can help to reduce students' FLCA (Duxbury and Tsai, 2010; Semmar, 2010). For example, Semmar (2010) suggest that students organize collaborative learning group with students who experience high levels of FLCA so that they can learn about the experiences, concerns and challenges they face in their foreign language classrooms. Cooperative learning is an important component to classroom learning because it provides students with opportunities to practice the target language and form positive peer relationships, and it helps create a stimulating environment (Duxbury and Tsai, 2010).

Further, Huang et al. (2010) confirmed that peer support is essential in reducing students' FLCA. This is because students spend considerable time together learning the same language and encounter similar language-learning difficulties. Language learners may receive support from their classmates not only in the form of friendship but also in ways that facilitate learning (von Wörde, 1998). Therefore, peer support has greater reciprocity because peers share equal status (Cauce et al., 1982; Hartup, 1989; Wentzel, 1994). Huang et al. (2010) studied a total of 158 freshmen students at a university in Taiwan who shared the same cultural and linguistic background. The participants were asked to complete three questionnaires: A background questionnaire, the FLCAS (Horwitz, Horwitz, and Cope, 1986) and the Classroom Life Measure.

Results show that academic and personal support from peers was positively correlated with students' comfort with English-language learning. The implications of their study show that a warm and accepting environment, as well as a positive relationship between teacher and student, is important for reducing anxiety and encouraging learning. Teachers should also encourage healthy relationships among peers (Huang et. al, 2010).

Finally, as Dewaele et al. (2008) suggested, for students who are majoring in a foreign language, studying abroad seems help reduce their FLCA. It helps foreign language students experience the target culture first-hand, which can in turn help increase their understanding and respect for the foreign language and culture. An "extended overseas experience in the target language country seems to increase self-confidence in it and, as a result, decrease foreign language classroom anxiety" (p.915).

Brief Description of Methodology Two Studies Used to Examine Student Responsibilities

As mentioned in Chapter 3, both empirical studies included in this book examined students' perspectives of their responsibilities for reducing their own FLCA. The first study involved 419 Chinese freshmen students at two major comprehensive universities in Beijing. The second study involved 436 Chinese freshmen students at one major language university in Beijing.

An expanded FLCAS (Horwitz et al., 1986) (see appendix A) was employed as the survey instrument. The expanded FLCAS included the original 33 items, a demographic information section and three open-ended questions. The expanded FLCAS was first translated into Chinese (see appendix B). The Chinese-language version of the FLCAS was then checked through back-translation, and it was finally pilot tested prior to administration.

The second open-ended question asked about participants' perspectives of what they can do to reduce their own FLCA. The data obtained from the participants' responses to the second open-ended question were analyzed identically for both studies. Specifically, their responses to the second open-ended question were sorted and categorized, and major recurring themes were identified and analyzed, with each theme representing a major student responsibility for reducing FLCA.

Three Major Student Responsibilities Reported by the First Study

As mentioned above, 419 freshmen students from two major comprehensive universities in Beijing, China participated in the first study. Among the 419 participants, 99 (23.6%) were English majors and 320 (76.4%) were non-English majors; 221 (52.7%) were male and 198 (47.3%) were female students. The second open-ended question on the expanded FLCAS asked the participants what they could do to reduce their own FLCA. Of the 419 participants, 330 (78.8%) answered this question and made a total of 529 individual responses. These 529 individual responses were further sorted into different categories, with each category representing a major responsibility they can take for reducing their own FLCA.

Table 23. Major Student Responsibilities for Reducing FLCA from the First Study: Total Number and Percentage of Responses

Responsibility	Gender		Major		Total
	Male	Female	English	Non-English	
Outside-the-classroom responsibilities	193 (81.8%)	242 (82.6%)	126 (80.8%)	309 (82.8%)	435 (82.2%)
Changing attitude toward language/course	29 (12.3%)	23 (7.8%)	9 (5.8%)	43 (11.5%)	52 (9.8%)
Inside-the-classroom responsibilities	14 (5.9%)	28 (9.6%)	21 (13.5%)	21 (5.6%)	42 (7.9%)
Subtotal	236 (100%)	293 (100%)	156 (100%)	373 (100%)	529 (100%)
Total Responses	529		529		529

The following three major student responsibilities for reducing their own FLCA were reported from the first study: a) outside-the-classroom responsibilities, b) changing attitude toward the language/course, and c) inside-the- classroom responsibilities. Table 23 presents a summary of these student responsibilities. It shows the total number and percentage of responses that fits into each category, sorted by gender (male vs. female) as well as by major (English vs. non-English).

As shown in Table 23, the reported three major student responsibilities, which were ranked from the most responses to the least, are: a) outside-the-classroom responsibilities (82.2%), b) changing attitude toward language/course (9.8%), and c) inside-the-classroom responsibilities (7.9%). Male participants ranked the three major student responsibilities in the same order, whereas female participants ranked "inside-the-classroom responsibilities" (9.6%) the second and "changing attitude toward language/course" (7.8%) the third. Similarly, non-English majors ranked the three major student responsibilities in the same order, whereas English majors ranked "inside-the-classroom responsibilities" (13.5%) the second and "changing attitude toward language/course" (5.8%) the third. Overall, "outside-the-classroom responsibilities" were overwhelmingly ranked as the largest category of student responsibilities for reducing their own FLCA with a total number of 435 (82.2%) responses.

Outside-the-classroom Responsibilities

The outside-the-classroom responsibilities were ranked as the most important responsibilities that Chinese freshmen students need to take for reducing their own FLCA. As shown in Table 23, a total of 435 individual responses were under this category. Despite the fact that there were slightly more male than female participants, i.e., among 419 participants, 221 (52.7%) were male and 198 (47.3%) female students, male participants (with 193 responses) made slightly fewer responses than female participants (with 242 responses). However, due to the different number of participants, i.e., among 419 participants, 99 (23.6%) were English majors and 320 (76.4%) non-English majors, English majors (with 126 responses) made approximately one-and–a-half times fewer responses than non-English majors (with 309 responses). These results suggest that both gender and major groups of participants agreed that their outside-the-classroom responsibilities became the largest major type of responsibility. Outside-the-classroom responsibilities, as reflected in their responses, include making adequate class preparation, ensuring plenty of language practice, and reviewing after class. Sample responses under this category include "be well prepared," "practice, practice, and practice," "study harder," and "review after class."

Changing Attitude toward Language/Course

Changing attitude toward language/course was ranked as the second major responsibility that Chinese freshmen students need to take for reducing their own FLCA. As shown in Table 23, a total of 52 individual responses were under this category. Due to the fact that there were slightly more male than female participants, i.e., among 419 participants, 221 (52.7%) were male and 198 (47.3%) female students, male participants (with 29 responses) made slightly more responses than female participants (with 23 responses). However, due to the different number of participants, i.e., among 419 participants, 99 (23.6%) were English majors and 320 (76.4%) non-English majors, English majors (with nine responses) made approximately four times fewer responses than non-English majors (with 43 responses). These results suggest that both gender and major groups of participants agreed that they should change their attitudes toward English language/course, which indicates showing more interest in learning English, becoming less worried about making mistakes, and building self-confidence, as reflected in their responses. Sample responses under this category include "become more interested in English," "try not to afraid of making mistakes and losing face," "not to worry about what others think," and "become more self-confident in learning English."

Inside-the-classroom Responsibilities

The inside-the-classroom responsibilities were ranked as the third major type of responsibility that Chinese freshmen students need to take for reducing their own FLCA. As shown in Table 23, a total of 42 individual responses were under this category. Despite the fact that there were slightly more male than female participants, i.e., among 419 participants, 221 (52.7%) were male and 198 (47.3%) female students, male participants (with 14 responses) made one time fewer responses than female participants (with 28 responses). However, English majors (with 21 responses) made exactly the same number of responses as non-English majors (with 21 responses), even though there were almost three-and-a-half times as many female participants as male participants, i.e., among 419 participants, 99 (23.6%) were English majors and 320 (76.4%) non-English majors. These results indicate a large difference across both gender and language groups of participants in terms of the number of responses made. Inside-the-classroom responsibilities, as reflected in their responses, include becoming more active in classroom participation, being more attentive, and feeling less anxious and worried about making mistakes and being laughed at by peers. Sample responses under this category include "pay attention to the teacher," "be active in answering questions," "don't be afraid of being laughed at by peers," and "volunteer to participate in class."

Three Major Student Responsibilities Reported by the Second Study

Four hundred and thirty-six freshmen students participated in the second study. Among the 436 participants, 171 (39%) were English majors, 111 (26%) majoring in other Western languages including French, Spanish, and German, and 154 (35%) majoring in non-Western languages Japanese, Korean, and Arabic. Of the 436 participants, 97 (22%) were male and 339 (78%) were female students. Like the first empirical study, the participants of the second study were asked to complete the expanded FLCAS. The second open-ended question on the expanded FLCAS asked the participants what they could do to reduce their FLCA. Of the 436 participants, 331 (75.9%) answered this question and made a total of 540 individual responses. These 540 individual responses were further sorted into different categories, with each category representing a major type of responsibility they can take for reducing their own FLCA.

Like the first study, the following three major student responsibilities for reducing their own FLCA were reported from the second study: a) outside-the-classroom responsibilities, b) changing attitude toward the language/course, and c) inside-the- classroom responsibilities. Table 24 presents a summary of these student responsibilities. It shows the total number and percentage of responses that fit into each category, sorted by gender (male vs. female) as well as by language (English vs. other Western languages vs. non-Western languages).

As shown in Table 24, the reported three major types of student responsibilities, which were ranked from the most responses to the least, are: a) outside-the-classroom responsibilities (74.4%), b) changing attitude toward language/course (14.6%), and c) inside-the-classroom responsibilities (10.9%). Female participants ranked the three major types of student responsibilities in the same order, whereas male participants ranked "inside-the-classroom responsibilities" (16.8%) the second and "changing attitude toward

Table 24. Major Student Responsibilities for Reducing FLCA from the Second Study: Total Number and Percentage of Responses

	Gender		Language			
Responsibility	Male	Female	English	Other Western	Non-Western	Total
Outside-the-classroom responsibilities	75 (74.3%)	327 (74.5%)	168 (65.9%)	130 (79.8%)	104 (85.2%)	402 (74.4%)
Changing attitude toward language/course	9 (8.9%)	70 (15.9%)	52 (20.4%)	21 (12.9%)	6 (4.9%)	79 (14.6%)
Inside-the-classroom responsibilities	17 (16.8%)	42 (9.6%)	35 (13.7%)	12 (7.4%)	12 (9.8%)	59 (10.9%)
Subtotal	101 (100%)	439 (100%)	255 (100%)	163 (100%)	122 (100%)	540 (100%)
Total Responses	540		540			540

language/course" (8.9%) the third. Similarly, participants majoring in English and other Western languages ranked the three major types of student responsibilities in the same order, whereas participants majoring in non-Western languages ranked "inside-the-classroom responsibilities" (9.8%) the second and "changing attitude toward language/course" (4.9%) the third. Overall, "outside-the-classroom responsibilities" were overwhelmingly ranked as the largest category of student responsibilities for reducing their own FLCA with a total number of 402 (74.4%) responses.

Outside-the-classroom Responsibilities

The outside-the-classroom responsibilities were ranked as the most important responsibilities that Chinese freshmen students need to take for reducing their own FLCA. As shown in Table 24, a total of 402 individual responses were under this category. Due to the different number of participants, i.e., among 436 participants, 97 (22%) were male and 339 (78%) were female participants, male participants (with 75 responses) made over three times fewer responses than female participants (with 327 responses). Obviously, English major participants (with 168 responses) made far more responses than those participants majoring in other Western languages (with 130 responses) and non-Western languages (104 responses), which might be due to different number of participants across the language group, i.e., among the 436 participants, 171 (39%) were English majors, 111 (26%) were majoring in other Western languages, and 154 (35%) were majoring in non-Western languages. These results suggest that both gender and language groups of participants agreed that their outside-the-classroom responsibilities became the largest major type of responsibilities. Outside-the-classroom responsibilities, as reflected in their responses, include making adequate class preparation, ensuring plenty of language practice, and reviewing after class. Sample responses under this category include "be well prepared," "practice, practice, and practice," "study harder," and "review after class."

Changing Attitude toward Language/Course

Changing attitude toward language/course was ranked as the second major responsibility that Chinese freshmen students need to take for reducing their own FLCA. As shown in Table 24, a total of 79 individual responses were under this category. Due to the different number of participants, i.e., among 436 participants, 97 (22%) were male and 339 (78%) were female participants, male participants (with nine responses) made over six times fewer responses than female participants (with 70 responses). English major participants (with 52 responses) made one time more responses than those participants majoring in other Western languages (with 21 responses) and more than seven times more responses than participants majoring in non-Western languages (six responses), even though the number of participants did not vary considerably across the language group, i.e., among the 436 participants, 171 (39%) were English majors, 111 (26%) were majoring in other Western languages, and 154 (35%) were majoring in non-Western languages. These results did indicate a large difference across both gender and language groups of participants. Changing attitude toward foreign language/course indicates that Chinese freshmen students should show more interest in learning the foreign language, become less worried about making mistakes, and build self-confidence, as reflected in their responses. Sample responses under this category include "become more interested in the foreign language," "try not to afraid of making mistakes and losing face," "not to worry about what others think," and "become more self-confident in learning the foreign language."

Inside-the-classroom Responsibilities

Inside-the-classroom responsibilities were ranked as the third major responsibility that Chinese freshmen students need to take for reducing their own FLCA. As shown in Table 24, a total of 59 individual responses were under this category. Due to the different number of participants, i.e., among 436 participants, 97 (22%) were male and 339 (78%) were female participants, male participants (with 17 responses) made one-and-a-half times fewer responses than female participants (with 42 responses). English major participants (with 35 responses) made approximately two times more responses than those participants majoring in other Western languages (with 12 responses) and non-Western languages (12 responses), even though the number of participants did not vary considerably across the language group, i.e., among the 436 participants, 171 (39%) were English majors; 111 (26%) majoring in other Western languages; and 154 (35%) majoring in non-Western languages. These results did indicate large difference across both gender and language groups of participants. Inside-the-classroom responsibilities, as reflected in their responses, indicate that Chinese freshmen students should become more active in classroom participation, be more attentive in class, and feel less anxious and worried about making mistakes and being laughed at by peers. Sample responses under this category include "pay attention to the teacher," "be active in answering questions in class," "don't be afraid of being laughed at by peers," and "volunteer to participate in class."

Similarities and Differences between the Two Studies

As shown in Table 25, there were two major similarities and two major differences in reporting student responsibilities for reducing their FLCA between the two empirical studies. First, overall, both studies reported the identical three types of student responsibilities and in the same ranking order: a) outside-the-classroom responsibilities, b) changing attitude toward the language/course, and c) inside-the-classroom responsibilities.

Second, despite the fact that there were a similar number of male and female participants in the first study and there were three times more female than male participants in the second study, both studies found large gender and major/language differences in terms of total number of responses for certain types of student responsibilities. In the first study, for the category of "inside-the-classroom responsibilities," large differences were found across gender and language groups of participants in terms of the number of responses made. In the second study, for categories of "changing attitude toward language/course" and "inside-the-classroom responsibilities," large differences were found across gender and language groups of participants in terms of the number of responses made.

Third, in the first study, a difference was found between male and female students in terms of the order of the three major types of student responsibilities for reducing their FLCA. Male participants ranked the three major types of student responsibilities in the same order, whereas female participants ranked "inside-the-classroom responsibilities" as the second and "changing attitude toward language/course" as the third.

Finally, in the second study, a difference was also found between male and female students in terms of the order of the three major types of student responsibilities for reducing their FLCA. Female participants ranked the three major types of student responsibilities in the same order, whereas male participants ranked "inside-the-classroom responsibilities" as the second and "changing attitude toward language/course" as the third.

Table 25. Similarities and Differences in Reporting Student Responsibilities between the Two Studies

Similarities	Differences
1. Overall, both studies reported the identical three types of student responsibilities, and in the same ranking order.	1. In the first study, male participants ranked the three major types of student responsibilities in the same order, whereas female participants ranked them differently.
2. Both studies found large gender and major/language differences in terms of total number of responses for certain types of student responsibilities.	2. In the second study, female participants ranked the three major types of student responsibilities in the same order, whereas male participants ranked them differently.

CONCLUSION

This chapter discussed the major responsibilities that foreign language students should take to reduce their FLCA. As described in the literature (Cauce et al., 1982; Crookall and Oxford, 1991; Dewaele et al., 2008; Donley, 1996; Foss and Reitzel, 1988; Hartup, 1989; Huang et al., 2010; Nakatani, 2010; Noormohamadi, 2009; Semmar, 2010; von Wörde, 1998; Wentzel, 1994; Young, 1991), students should take certain responsibilities to alleviate their FLCA. For example, they should be aware of the types of anxiety they face in the foreign language classrooms and try to reduce their FLCA in order to manage and take control of their foreign language learning; further, they should become familiar with their own language-learning styles and develop strategies that reduce their anxiety and facilitate their foreign language learning in the classroom. In addition, they should organize collaborative learning groups with students who experience high levels of FLCA so that they can learn about the experiences, concerns and challenges they face in their foreign language classrooms (Semmar, 2010). The chapter presented the results of the two empirical studies included in this book. These results have provided important implications for Chinese freshmen students learning foreign languages at universities.

REFERENCES

Cauce, A. M., Felner, R. D., and Primavera, J. (1982). Social support in high-risk adolescents: Structural components and adaptive impact. *American Journal of Community Psychology*, 10, 417–428.

Crookall, D., and Oxford, R. (1991). Dealing with anxiety: Some practical activities for language learners and teacher trainees. In E. K. Horwitz and D. J. Young (Eds.), *Language anxiety: From theory and research to classroom implications* (pp. 141-150). Englewood Cliffs, NJ: Prentice-Hall.

Dewaele, J-M., Petrides, K. V., and Furnham, A. (2008). Effects of trait emotional intelligence and sociobiographical variables on communicative anxiety and foreign language anxiety among multilinguals: A review and empirical investigation. *Language and Learning, 59,* 911-960.

Donley, P. M. (1996). Ten ways to cope with foreign language anxiety. *The Forum of Phi Sigma Iota, 8*(1), 13.

Duxbury, J. G. and Tsai, L. L. (2010). The effects of cooperative learning on foreign language anxiety: A comparative study of Taiwanese and American universities. *International Journal of Instruction, 3*(1), 3-18.

Foss, K. A., and Reitzel, A. C. (1988). A relational model for managing second language anxiety. *TESOL Quarterly, 20*, 559-562.

Hartup, W. W. (1989). Social relationships and their development significance. *American Psychologist*, 44, 120-126.

Horwitz, E. K., Horwitz, M. B., and Cope, J. A. (1986). Foreign language classroom anxiety. *The Modern Language Journal, 70*, 125-132.

Huang, S., Eslami, Z., and Hu, R. J. S. (2010). The relationship between teacher and peer support and English-language learners' anxiety. *English Language Teaching, 3*(1), 32-40.

Nakatani, Y. (2010). Identifying strategies that facilitate EFL learners' oral communication: A classroom study using multiple data collection procedures. *The Modern Language Journal, 94*(1), 116-136.

Noormohamadi, R. (2009). On the relationship between language learning strategies and foreign language anxiety. *Journal of Pan-Pacific Association of Applied Linguistics, 13*(1), 39-52.

Rubin, J., and Thompson, I. (1982). *How to be a more successful language learner*. Boston: Heinle and Heinle.

Semmar, Y. (2010). First-year university students and language anxiety: Insights into the English version of the Foreign Language Classroom Anxiety Scale. *The International Journal of Learning, 17*(1), 81-93.

von Wörde, R. (1998). *An investigation of students' perspectives on foreign language anxiety. Unpublished doctoral dissertation*. George Mason University, Fairfax, Virginia.

Wentzel, K. R. (1994). Relations of social goal pursuit to social acceptance, classroom behavior, and perceived social support. *Journal of Educational Psychology*, 86, 173-182.

Young, D. (1991). The relationship between anxiety and foreign language oral proficiency rating. In E. K. Horwitz., and D. J. Young, (Eds.). *Language anxiety: From theory and research to classroom implications* (pp.57-63). Englewood Cliffs, N.J.: Prentice Hall.

Chapter 9

TEACHERS' RESPONSIBILITIES FOR REDUCING STUDENTS' FOREIGN LANGUAGE CLASSROOM ANXIETY

ABSTRACT

Research has shown that teachers can create foreign language classroom anxiety (FLCA) for their students, and therefore should be responsible for reducing their students' FLCA (Abu-Rabia, 2004; Casado and Dereshiwsky, 2001; Chen and Chang, 2004; Ewald, 2007; Kim, 2009; Lucas, 1984; Onwuegbuzie, Bailey, and Daley, 1997; Wu, 2010; Yan and Horwitz, 2008; Young, 1990; Zhao, 2007). Many studies indicate that foreign language teachers employ instruction strategies and create a low-anxiety or anxiety-free environment in order to facilitate students' foreign language learning in the classroom. For example, Lucas (1984) suggested the teachers create a warm, easy-going atmosphere in the classroom so that students are relaxed and feel less anxious about learning the language. Furthermore, Young (1990) argued that the instructor's relaxed and positive error-correction attitude can greatly reduce students' FLCA. One way to provide correction input without much anxiety is, as indicated by Young (1990), to "model students' responses, that is, simply repeat the correct version of what the students are attempting to say" (p. 550); in addition, the teacher's "positive, friendly and relaxed general attitude toward students" (p. 551) can help reduce students' FLCA.

This chapter discusses foreign language teachers' responsibilities for reducing their students' FLCA. It first briefly summarizes the previous literature. As mentioned in Chapter 3, both empirical studies included in this book examined teachers' responsibilities for reducing their students'

FLCA as reported by the Chinese university freshmen students. This chapter then briefly describes the research methodology that both studies used to examine teacher responsibilities for alleviating their students' FLCA. Further, it reports the research findings of both studies. Finally, this chapter discusses the similarities and differences in reporting teacher responsibilities for reducing their students' FLCA between the two empirical studies.

BRIEF SUMMARY OF PREVIOUS LITERATURE

Many studies have examined foreign language teachers' responsibilities for reducing their students' FLCA. This section summarizes the previous literature by briefly reviewing a selection of eight studies, in a chronological order, which were conducted in the last decade (Abu-Rabia, 2004; Casado and Dereshiwsky, 2001; Chen and Chang, 2004; Ewald, 2007; Kim, 2009; Wu, 2010; Yan and Horwitz, 2008; Zhao, 2007).

Approximately a decade ago, Casado and Dereshiwsky (2001) identified and compared the perceptions of first- and second-semester university students towards feelings of anxiety experienced during foreign language learning as measured by the FLCAS scale (Horwitz, Horwitz, and Cope, 1986). The participants were 114 students learning Spanish in their first semester at an American university and 169 students learning Spanish in their second semester at the same university. The study provided the following three affective techniques to alleviate feelings of anxiety cited by modern-language teaching experts: "Making students aware that being fluent and getting a good accent in the target language take in most cases several years of study and practice; providing students with positive reinforcement and creating a relaxed classroom environment; helping students that have a mental block towards language learning by providing them with out-of-the-classroom individual assistance"(p. 549). In addition, they suggested the following four teaching methods to reduce students' FLCA: "Conducting class activities in groups; explaining grammar concepts in beginning and elementary classes in the native, not in the target language; forming support groups for performance-concerned students so they can discuss concerns and difficulties encountered in language learning; using smaller classes to help instructors identify students experiencing anxiety and give them special attention and support"(p. 549).

Three years later, Abu-Rabia (2004) investigated the perceptions of 67 seventh-grade students who were learning English as a foreign language at two religious schools in Israel of how teachers' attitudes impact their FLCA. The results show that teachers' attitudes were negatively and significantly correlated with FLCA. In other words, the higher the students' evaluation of their teachers as "supportive, encouraging, and understanding" (p. 719), the lower the students' level of FLCA. Therefore, teachers should create a supportive and friendly classroom learning environment for students.

In the same year, Chen and Chang (2004) investigated the possible causal relationship between FLCA and language-learning difficulties experienced by 1,187 students from ten universities and colleges around Taiwan and provided very important implications for foreign language teachers. For example, foreign language teachers should first aim at improving their students' self-perception of proficiency by focusing on positive experiences. Further, foreign language teachers should be patient and supportive in the classroom. Third, for students with classroom learning difficulties, foreign language teachers need to "adopt teaching-learning approaches that will effectively address these specific difficulties" (p. 285) and so alleviate FLCA.

Later, through a qualitative analysis of questionnaire data obtained from 21 advanced students of Spanish, Ewald (2007) examined FLCA in the context of upper-level language classrooms. The results indicate many of these students experienced FLCA in upper-level classes. Students pointed to the key role of the teacher in producing and relieving FLCA. The study provided many suggestions for teachers to reduce students' FLCA in advanced foreign language classrooms. For example, teachers should build advanced students' confidence and self-perception. Convince them that the "challenge of learning to use a foreign language is not outside their grasp" (p. 134). Assure them that "mistakes are normal and expected and that even through flawed participation they learn" (p. 134). Further, teachers should encourage students to participate but not force them to speak. Finally, the teacher should discuss FLCA in class and help to alleviate students' FLCA through peer support.

Zhao (2007) examined high school students' English learning anxiety in Chinese English-as-a-foreign-language (EFL) classrooms. In total, 115 students from a high school in China were asked to complete the FLCAS (Horwitz et al., 1986). This study offered the following suggestions for teachers to alleviate students' FLCA. First, teachers should create a relaxed atmosphere for students so that they can feel safe or comfortable to speak in class. Second, teachers should avoid negative evaluation of students in the classroom and use positive comments on students' behaviors. Third, teachers should stop focusing students' attention on exams by not ranking students by their examination scores. Finally, teachers can also "explicitly tell students the inevitability of the existence of anxiety in English learning and let them know that anxiety can be reduced through the self-regulation of their thinking and study" (p. 30).

Recently, Yan and Horwitz (2008) examined Chinese university students' perceptions of how FLCA works together with other variables in influencing their English language learning. They suggested that teachers should encourage students to discuss language-learning strategies and guide them to select specific learning strategies. Further, teachers should group students of similar levels together and provide them with appropriate materials in order to reduce pressure from comparison with peers. Finally, class activities could be designed to encourage cooperation instead of competition, and adequate time for pair or group discussion could be allowed before oral responses are required. In "raising students' interest and motivation, more tedious classroom tasks (such as listening to the tapes and answering questions) could be broken into several shorter sections and a greater proportion of interesting authentic materials—songs, magazines, and movies—could be employed" (p. 175).

Recently, Kim (2009) examined 59 Korean college students' FLCA in the context of learning English as a foreign language and suggested several teaching implications for reducing FLCA. First, Kim (2009) suggests that foreign language teachers should "incorporate pair or group work and games into language instruction to reduce student anxiety associated with public performance and improvisation" (p. 154). Further, the teacher could use meaningful tasks and familiar topics in communicative settings because they may contribute to increasing the comfort level among foreign language learners. Finally, teachers could teach students effective strategies to copy with their FLCA.

Most recently, Wu (2010) examined the relationship between FLCA and learning strategies in the English language classrooms. Sixty-six Chinese adult learners of English (all major students) from a university in Taiwan participated in the study. Wu (2010) argued that it is the language instructors' mission to reduce their students' FLCA and accelerate their learning. On the one hand, the teachers need to "create a less threatening atmosphere, to motivate, and to strengthen student confidence" (p. 184); on the other hand, teachers need to teach their students effective language-learning strategies in order to accelerate their learning. However, students themselves should also develop their own language-learning strategies, which can lower their FLCA level.

Brief Description of Methodology Two Studies Used to Examine Teacher Responsibilities

As mentioned in Chapter 3, both empirical studies included in this book examined students' perspectives of their foreign language teachers' responsibilities for reducing students' FLCA. The first study involved 419 Chinese freshmen students at two major comprehensive universities in Beijing. The second study involved 436 Chinese freshmen students at one major language university in Beijing.

An expanded FLCAS (Horwitz et al., 1986) (see appendix A) was employed as the survey instrument. The expanded FLCAS included the original 33 items, a demographic information section and three open-ended questions. The expanded FLCAS was first translated into Chinese (see appendix B). The Chinese-language version of the FLCAS was then checked through back-translation, and it was finally pilot tested prior to administration.

The final open-ended question asked about participants' perspectives of what their foreign language teachers can do to reduce students' FLCA. The data obtained from the participants' responses to the final open-ended question were analyzed identically for both studies. Specifically, their responses to the third open-ended question were sorted and categorized, and major recurring themes were identified and analyzed with each theme representing a major teacher responsibility for reducing students' FLCA.

Four Major Teacher Responsibilities Reported by the First Study

Four hundred and nineteen freshmen students from two major comprehensive universities in Beijing participated in the first study. Among the 419 participants, 99 (23.6%) were English majors and 320 (76.4%) were non-English majors; 221 (52.7%) were male and 198 (47.3%) were female students. The final open-ended question on the expanded FLCAS asked the participants what they thought their foreign language teachers could do to reduce their FLCA. Of the 419 participants, 285 (68%) answered this question and made a total of 397 responses. These 397 individual responses were further sorted into different categories, with each category representing a major role that foreign language classroom teachers could take in helping their students reduce FLCA.

The following four major teacher responsibilities for reducing their students' FLCA were reported from the first study: a) improving teaching methods, b) changing attitude toward students, c) creating supportive classroom environment, and d) adjusting language use. Table 26 presents a summary of these responsibilities. It shows the total number and percentage of responses that fits into each category, sorted by gender (male vs. female) as well as by major (English vs. non-English).

As shown in Table 26, the reported four major teacher responsibilities, which were ranked from the most response to the least, are: a) improving teaching methods (46.3%), b) changing attitude toward students (21.9%), c) creating supportive classroom environment (19.9%), and d) adjusting language use (11.8%). Female participants ranked the four major teacher responsibilities in the same order, whereas male participants ranked "creating supportive classroom environment" (19.3%) the second and "changing attitude toward students" (18.7%) the third. Similarly, non-English majors ranked the four teacher responsibilities in the same order, whereas English majors ranked "creating supportive classroom environment" (28.9%) as the second and "changing attitude toward students" (19%) as the third. "

Table 26. Major Teacher Responsibilities for Reducing Students' FLCA from the First Study: Total Number and Percentage of Responses

Teacher Responsibility	Gender		Major		Total
	Male	Female	English	Non-English	
Improving teaching methods	80 (48.2%)	104 (45%)	50 (41.3%)	134 (48.6%)	184 (46.3%)
Changing attitudes toward students	31 (18.7%)	56 (24.2%)	23 (19%)	64 (23.2%)	87 (21.9%)
Creating supportive classroom environment	32 (19.3%)	47 (20.3%)	35 (28.9%)	44 (15.9%)	79 (19.9%)
Adjusting language use	23 (13.9%)	24 (10.4%)	13 (10.7%)	34 (12.3%)	47 (11.8%)
Subtotal	166 (100%)	231 (100%)	121 (100%)	276 (100%)	397 (100%)
Total Responses	397		397		397

"Improving teaching methods" was consistently ranked as the first teacher responsibility across both gender and major groups, while "adjusting language use" was repeatedly ranked as the fourth.

Improving Teaching Methods

Improving teaching methods was ranked as the most important teacher responsibility for helping their students reduce FLCA. As shown in Table 26, a total of 184 individual responses were under this category. Despite the fact that there were slightly more male than female participants, i.e., among 419 participants, 221 (52.7%) were male and 198 (47.3%) female students, male participants (with 80 responses) made slightly fewer responses than female participants (with 104 responses). However, due to the different number of participants, i.e., among 419 participants, 99 (23.6%) were English majors and 320 (76.4%) were non-English majors, English majors (with 50 responses) made over one-and-a-half times fewer responses than non-English majors (with 134 responses). These results suggest that both gender and major groups of participants agreed that the most important thing that foreign language teachers could do to help reduce their students' FLCA was to improve their teaching methods. Improving teaching methods, as reflected in the responses, suggests that teachers use student-centered approaches to creating more opportunities for students to practice English listening and speaking. Sample responses under this category include "student-centered, not teacher-centered teaching," "play English movies," "focus on listening and speaking," and "create more opportunities for students to practice."

Changing Attitude toward Students

Changing attitude toward students was ranked as the second most important teacher responsibility for helping their students reduce FLCA. As shown in Table 26, a total of 87 individual responses were under this category. Despite the fact that there were slightly more male than female participants, i.e., among 419 participants, 221 (52.7%) were male and 198 (47.3%) were female students, male participants (with 31 responses) made fewer responses than female participants (with 56 responses). However, due to the different number of participants, i.e., among 419 participants, 99 (23.6%) were English majors and 320 (76.4%) were non-English majors, English majors (with 23 responses) made approximately two times fewer responses than non-English majors (with 64 responses). These results suggest that both gender and major groups of participants agreed that the second most important thing that foreign language teachers could do to help reduce their students' FLCA was to change their attitudes toward students. Changing attitudes toward students, as reflected in the responses, suggests that teachers encourage students to practice the language, praise students whenever they make an attempt in class, and become tolerant of students' mistakes. Sample responses under this category include "encourage students more," "praise students whenever they participate," and "have tolerance for students' mistakes."

Creating Supportive Classroom Environment

Creating a supportive classroom environment was ranked as the third most important teacher responsibility for helping their students reduce FLCA. As shown in Table 26, a total of 79 individual responses were under this category. Despite the fact that there were slightly more male than female participants, i.e., among 419 participants, 221 (52.7%) were male and 198 (47.3%) were female students, male participants (with 32 responses) made fewer responses than female participants (with 47 responses). However, English majors (with 35 responses) made slightly fewer responses than non-English majors (with 44 responses), although there were far more non-English major participants than English major participants, i.e., among 419 participants, 99 (23.6%) were English majors and 320 (76.4%) were non-English majors. These results suggest little difference in the number of responses across gender and major groups. Creating a supportive classroom environment, as reflected in the responses, suggests that teachers should be humorous and friendly, make the classroom a fun place for learning the foreign language, and create a relaxed and non-threatening classroom. Sample responses under this category include "be humorous and sympathetic," "make class more interesting," and "create a relaxed and friendly classroom."

Adjusting Language Use

Adjusting language use was ranked as the fourth most important teacher responsibility for helping their students reduce FLCA. As shown in Table 26, a total of 47 individual responses were under this category. Male (with 23 responses) and female (with 24 responses) participants made approximately the same number of responses although there were slightly more male than female participants. However, due to the fact that there were far more non-English major participants than English major participants, i.e., among 419 participants, 99 (23.6%) were English majors and 320 (76.4%) were non-English majors, English majors (with 13 responses) made approximately one-and–a-half times fewer responses than non-English majors (with 34 responses). These results suggest little difference in the number of responses across gender and major groups. Adjusting language use, as reflected in the responses, suggests that teachers use more English in class, speak more slowly and clearly, and use Chinese when necessary. Sample responses under this category include "use more English," "slow down rate of speech," "speak more clearly," and "use Chinese to explain difficult points."

Four Major Teacher Responsibilities Reported by the Second Study

Four hundred and thirty-six freshmen students participated in the second study. Among the 436 participants, 171 (39%) were English majors; 111 (26%) were majoring in other Western languages including French, Spanish, and German, and 154 (35%) were majoring in non-Western languages Japanese, Korean, and Arabic. Of the 436 participants, 97 (22%) were male and 339 (78%) were female students. Like the first empirical study, the participants of the second study were asked to complete the expanded FLCAS. The final open-ended question on the expanded FLCAS asked the participants what they thought their foreign language teachers could do to reduce their FLCA. Of the 436 participants, 286 (65.6%) answered this question and made a total of 483 responses. These 483 individual responses were further sorted into different categories, with each category representing a major role that foreign language classroom teachers could take in helping their students reduce FLCA.

The following four major teacher responsibilities for reducing their students' FLCA were reported from the second study: a) improving teaching methods, b) changing attitude toward students, c) creating supportive classroom environment, and d) adjusting language use. Table 27 presents a summary of these teacher responsibilities. It shows the total number and percentage of responses that fits into each category, sorted by gender (male vs. female) as well as by language (English vs. other Western languages vs. and non-Western languages).

As shown in Table 27, the reported four major teacher responsibilities, which were ranked from the most response to the least, are: a) improving teaching methods (37.1%), b) changing attitude toward students (34.8%), c) creating supportive classroom environment (23.6%), and d) adjusting language use (4.6%). Female participants ranked the four major teacher responsibilities in the same order, whereas male participants ranked "changing attitude toward students" (40.3%) as the first and "improving teaching methods" (29.9%) as the second. Similarly, participants majoring in English and other Western languages ranked the four major teacher responsibilities in the same order, whereas participants majoring in non-Western languages ranked "creating supportive classroom environment" (28.7%) as the second and "changing attitude toward student" (27.6%) as the third. Overall, "improving teaching methods" was consistently ranked as the first major teacher responsibility across both gender and major groups, with the exception of the male participants, who ranked "changing attitude toward students" (40.3%) as the first responsibility; while "adjusting language use" was repeatedly ranked as the fourth.

Improving Teaching Methods

Improving teaching methods was ranked as the most important teacher responsibility for helping their students reduce FLCA. As shown in Table 27, a total of 179 individual responses were under this category. Due to the different number of participants, i.e., among 436 participants, 97 (22%) were male and 339 (78%) were female participants, male participants (with 23 responses) made over six times fewer responses than female participants (with 156 responses). Obviously, English major participants (with 105 responses) made over one time more responses than those participants majoring in other Western languages (with 48 responses), and approximately three times more responses than participants majoring in non-Western languages (26 responses), although among the 436 participants, 171 (39%) were English majors; 111 (26%) were majoring in other Western languages, and 154 (35%) were majoring in non-Western languages. These results suggest little difference between male and female participants, but a large difference among participants majoring in English and those majoring in other Western languages and non-Western languages.

Table 27. Major Teacher Responsibilities for Reducing Students' FLCA from the Second Study: Total Number and Percentage of Responses

	Gender		Language			
Teacher Responsibility	Male	Female	English	Other Western	Non-Western	Total
Improving teaching methods	23 (29.9%)	156 (38.4%)	105 (39.3%)	48 (37.2%)	26 (29.9%)	179 (37.1%)
Changing attitudes toward students	31 (40.3%)	137 (33.7%)	98 (36.7%)	46 (35.7%)	24 (27.6%)	168 (34.8%)
Creating supportive classroom environments	15 (19.5%)	99 (24.4%)	62 (23.2%)	27 (20.9%)	25 (28.7%)	114 (23.6%)
Adjusting language use	8 (10.4%)	14 (3.4%)	2 (0.7%)	8 (6.2%)	12 (13.8%)	22 (4.6%)
Subtotal	77 (100%)	406 (100%)	267 (100%)	129 (100%)	87 (100%)	483 (100%)
Total Responses	483		483			483

Improving teaching methods, as reflected in the responses, suggests that teachers use student-centered approaches to create more opportunities for students to practice listening and speaking. Sample responses under this category include "student-centered, not teacher-centered teaching," "focus on listening and speaking," and "create more opportunities for students to practice the foreign language."

Changing Attitude toward Students

Changing attitude toward students was ranked as the second most important teacher responsibility for helping their students reduce FLCA. As shown in Table 27, a total of 168 individual responses were under this category. Due to the different number of participants, i.e., among 436 participants, 97 (22%) were male and 339 (78%) were female participants, male participants (with 31 responses) made over three times fewer responses than female participants (with 137 responses). Obviously, English major participants (with 98 responses) made over one time more responses than those participants majoring in other Western languages (with 46 responses), and over three times more responses than participants majoring in non-Western languages (24 responses), although among the 436 participants, 171 (39%) were English majors; 111 (26%) were majoring in other Western languages, and 154 (35%) were majoring in non-Western languages. These results suggest little difference between male and female participants, but a large difference among participants majoring in English and those majoring in other Western languages and non-Western languages. Changing attitude toward students, as reflected in the responses, suggests that teachers encourage students to practice the language, praise students whenever they make an attempt in class, and become tolerant of students' mistakes. Sample responses under this category include "encourage students more," "praise students whenever they participate," and "have tolerance for students' mistakes."

Creating Supportive Classroom Environment

Creating supportive classroom environment was ranked as the third most important teacher responsibility for helping their students reduce FLCA. As shown in Table 27, a total of 114 individual responses were under this category. Due to the different number of participants, i.e., among 436 participants, 97 (22%) were male and 339 (78%) were female participants, male participants (with 15 responses) made five times fewer responses than female participants (with 99 responses). English major participants (with 62 responses) made over one time more responses than those participants majoring in other Western languages (with 27 responses) and non-Western languages (25 responses), although among the 436 participants, 171 (39%) were English majors; 111 (26%) were majoring in other Western languages, and 154 (35%) were majoring in non-Western languages. These results suggest large differences in the number of responses across both gender and language groups. Creating a supportive classroom environment, as reflected in the responses, suggests that teachers should be humorous and friendly, make the classroom a fun place for learning the foreign language, and create a relaxed and non-threatening classroom. Sample responses under this category include "be humorous and sympathetic," "make class more interesting," and "create a relaxed and friendly classroom."

Adjusting Language Use

Adjusting language use was ranked as the fourth most important teacher responsibility for helping their students reduce FLCA. As shown in Table 27, a total of 22 individual responses were under this category. Due to the different number of participants, i.e., among 436 participants, 97 (22%) were male and 339 (78%) were female participants, male participants (with eight responses) made approximately one time fewer responses than female participants (with 14 responses). English major participants (with two responses) made three times fewer responses than those participants majoring in other Western languages (with eight responses), and five times fewer responses than participants majoring in non-Western languages (12 responses), although among the 436 participants, 171 (39%) were English majors; 111 (26%) were majoring in other Western languages, and 154 (35%) were majoring in non-Western languages. These results suggest large differences in the number of responses across both gender and language groups. Adjusting language use, as reflected in the responses, suggests that teachers use more foreign language in class, speak more slowly and clearly, and use Chinese when necessary. Sample responses under this category include "use more foreign language," "slow down rate of speech," "speak more clearly," and "use Chinese to explain difficult points."

SIMILARITIES AND DIFFERENCES BETWEEN THE TWO STUDIES

As shown in Table 28, there were two major similarities and two major differences in reporting teacher responsibility for helping reduce their students' FLCA. First, overall, both studies reported the identical four major teacher responsibilities and in the same ranking order: a) improving teaching methods, b) changing attitude toward students, c) creating supportive classroom environment, and d) adjusting language use.

Second, in both studies, "improving teaching methods" was consistently ranked as the first teacher responsibility across both gender and major groups, while "adjusting language use" was repeatedly ranked as the fourth.

Third, in both studies, ranking order difference was found across gender and major/language groups. In the first study, female participants ranked the four major teacher responsibilities in the same order, whereas male participants ranked "creating supportive classroom environment" as the second and "changing attitude toward students" as the third. Similarly, non-English majors ranked the four teacher responsibilities in the same order, whereas English majors ranked "creating supportive classroom environment" as the second and "changing attitude toward students" as the third.

Table 28. Similarities and Differences in Reporting Teacher Responsibilities between the Two Studies

Similarities	Differences
1. Overall, both studies reported the identical four major teacher roles, and in the same ranking order.	1. In both studies, ranking order difference was found across gender and major/language groups.
2. In both studies, "improving teaching methods" was consistently ranked as the first role across both gender and major groups, while "adjusting language use" was repeatedly ranked as the fourth.	2. In the first study, no large difference in the number of responses across gender and major groups was found; however, in the second study, large difference in the number of responses across gender and/or language groups was found for different response categories.

In the second study, female participants ranked the four major teacher responsibilities in the same order, whereas male participants ranked "changing attitude toward students" as the first and "improving teaching methods" as the second. Similarly, participants majoring in English and other Western languages ranked the four major teacher responsibilities in the same order, whereas participants majoring in non-Western languages ranked "creating supportive classroom environment" as the second and "changing attitude toward student" as the third.

Finally, in the first study, no large difference in the number of responses across gender and major groups was found; however, in the second study, a large difference in the number of responses across gender and/or language groups was found for different response categories. For example, for the first and second teacher responsibilities, little difference was found across the gender group but a large difference was found across the language group; for the third and fourth teacher responsibilities, a large difference was found for both gender and language groups.

Conclusion

This chapter discussed the major teacher responsibilities for reducing their students' FLCA. As described in the literature (Abu-Rabia, 2004; Casado and Dereshiwsky, 2001; Chen and Chang, 2004; Ewald, 2007; Kim, 2009; Lucas, 1984; Onwuegbuzie et al., 1997; Wu, 2010; Yan and Horwitz, 2008; Young, 1990; Zhao, 2007), foreign language teachers employ instruction strategies and create a low-anxiety or anxiety-free classroom environments in order to facilitate students' foreign language learning. For example, teachers should create a warm, easy-going atmosphere in the classroom so that students are relaxed and feel less anxious about learning the language (Lucas, 1984). Further, the teacher's "positive, friendly and relaxed general attitude toward students" (Young, 1990, p. 551) can help reduce students' FLCA. This chapter then presented the results of the two empirical studies included in this book. These results have provided important implications for Chinese teachers of foreign languages at universities.

References

Abu-Rabia, S. (2004). Teachers' role, learners' gender differences, and FL anxiety among seventh-grade students studying English as a FL. *Educational Psychology, 24*(5), 711-721.

Casado, M. A., and Dereshiwsky, M. I. (2001). Foreign language anxiety of university students. *College Student Journal, 35*, 539-551.

Chen, T. Y., and Chang, G. B. Y. (2004). The relationship between foreign language anxiety and learning difficulties. *Foreign Language Annals, 37*(2), 279–289.

Ewald, J. D. (2007). Foreign language learning anxiety in upper-level classes: Involving students as researchers. *Foreign Language Annals, 40*(1), 122–142.

Horwitz, E. K., Horwitz, M. B., and Cope, J. A. (1986). Foreign language classroom anxiety. *The Modern Language Journal, 70*, 125-132.

Kim, S. Y. (2009). Questioning the stability of foreign language classroom anxiety and motivation across different classroom contexts. *Foreign Language Annals, 42*(1), 138-157.

Lucas, J. (1984). Communication apprehension in the ESL classroom: Getting our students to talk. *Foreign Language Annals, 17*(6), 593–598.

Onwuegbuzie, A. J., Bailey, P., and Daley, C. E. (1997). *Foreign language anxiety among college students.* Paper presented at the Annual Meeting of the Mid-South Educational Research Association, Memphis, TN.

Wu, K. H. (2010). The relationship between language learners' anxiety and learning strategy in the CLT classrooms. *International Education Studies, 3*(1), 174-191.

Yan, J. X., and Horwitz, E. K. (2008). Learners' perceptions of how anxiety interacts with personal and instructional factors to influence their achievement in English: A qualitative analysis of EFL learners in China. *Language Learning, 58*(1), 151-183.

Young, D. J. (1990). An investigation of students' perspectives on anxiety and speaking. *Foreign Language Annals, 23*(6), 539-553.

Zhao, N. (2007). A study of high school students' English learning anxiety. *The Non-Western EFL Journal, 9*(3), 22-34.

APPENDIX A: THE EXPANDED FOREIGN LANGUAGE CLASSROOM ANXIETY SCALE (FLCAS)

INSTRUCTIONS

1. Please read each item carefully before you choose your answer.
2. Foreign language or language refers to the foreign language you are currently studying.
3. For items that refer to teacher(s), course(s), and class(es), please don't focus on any particular teacher(s), course(s), or class(es). Rather, think about your teachers, lectures, and classes in general.
4. SA= strongly agree; A= agree; N= neither agree nor disagree; D= disagree; SD= strongly disagree

I. Personal Information

Your Gender	Male ____ Female __
Your Major	______________________
Your Native Language	______________________
Foreign Language You are Studying	______________________
Starting Date of Learning that Language	______________________

II. Foreign Language Classroom Anxiety

No	Items	SD	D	N	A	SA	Comments
		1	2	3	4	5	
1	I never feel quite sure of myself when I am speaking in my foreign language class.						
2	I don't worry about making mistakes in language class.						
3	I tremble when I know that I'm going to be called on in language class.						
4	It frightens me when I don't understand what the teacher is saying in the foreign language.						
5	It wouldn't bother me at all to take more foreign language classes.						
6	During language class, I find myself thinking about things that have nothing to do with the course.						
7	I keep thinking that the other students are better at languages than I am.						
8	I am usually at ease during tests in my language class.						
9	I start to panic when I have to speak without preparation in language class.						
10	I worry about the consequences of failing my foreign language class.						
11	I don't understand why some people get so upset over foreign language classes.						
12	In language class, I can get so nervous I forget things I know.						
13	It embarrasses me to volunteer answers in my language class.						
14	I would not be nervous speaking the foreign language with native speakers.						
15	I get upset when I don't understand what the teacher is correcting.						
16	Even if I am well prepared for language class, I feel anxious about it.						
17	I often feel like not going to my language class.						
18	I feel confident when I speak in foreign language class.						
19	I am afraid that my language teacher is ready to correct every mistake I make.						
20	I can feel my heart pounding when I'm going to be called on in language class.						
21	The more I study for a language test, the more confused I get.						
22	I don't feel pressure to prepare very well for language class.						
23	I always feel that the other students speak the foreign language better than I do.						

No	Items	SD	D	N	A	SA	Comments
		1	2	3	4	5	
24	I feel very self-conscious about speaking the foreign language in front of other students.						
25	Language class moves so quickly I worry about getting left behind.						
26	I feel more tense and nervous in my language class than in my other classes.						
27	I get nervous and confused when I am speaking in my language class.						
28	When I'm on my way to language class, I feel very sure and relaxed.						
29	I get nervous when I don't understand every word the language teacher says.						
30	I feel overwhelmed by the number of rules you have to learn to speak a foreign language.						
31	I am afraid that the other students will laugh at me when I speak the foreign language.						
32	I would probably feel comfortable around native speakers of the foreign language.						
33	I get nervous when the language teacher asks questions I haven't prepared in advance.						

III. Open-Ended Questions

1. Why do you feel anxious in your foreign language classroom?

2. What can you do to reduce your foreign language classroom anxiety (FLCA)?

3. What can your foreign language teacher(s) do to reduce your FLCA?

Thanks for your participation!

Appendix B: The Expanded Foreign Language Classroom Anxiety Scale (FLCAS) (Chinese Version)

外语课堂焦虑问卷

说明：

1. 选择答案之前请仔细看题。
2. 问卷中的“外语”或者“语言”就是你现在所学的那门外语。
3. 问卷中提到教师、课程、课堂时，选择答案时请考虑你学习该门外语的总体情况，而不要集中考虑某个具体的教师、课程和课堂
4. 1 = 非常反对； 2 = 反对； 3 = 既不赞同也不反对； 4 = 赞同； 5 = 非常赞同。

I. 个人基本情况

性别　　男 ________ 女 ________

专业 ____________________

母语 ____________________

正在学习的外语 ____________________

开始学习那门外语的具体时间 ____________________

II. 外语课堂焦虑单选题

题号	问题	1	2	3	4	5	说明
1	我在外语课堂上说外语时，从不自信。						
2	我在外语课堂上不担心犯错。						
3	我在外语课堂上当知道老师会叫到我时感到焦虑。						
4	当我听不懂老师用外语讲课时我感到惊恐。						
5	我对上更多的外语课不感到烦心。						
6	我在外语课堂上发现自己想些与课程无关的事情。						
7	我总认为别人的外语比我好。						
8	在参加外语课堂上的考试时我通常感到轻松。						
9	在外语课堂上不做准备就讲外语时我感到恐慌。						
10	我担心外语课程不及格会带来不好的后果。						
11	我不明白为什么有些人在外语课堂上感到心烦不安。						
12	在外语课堂上我想不起我知道的东西时就紧张。						
13	在外语课堂上当我自愿回答问题时觉得不好意思。						
14	与讲该门外语的本国人讲外语时我不会紧张。						
15	当老师纠错我不明白时就感到心烦。						
16	即使我做好了充分准备，我上外语课时还会担心。						
17	我经常不想去上外语课。						
18	在外语课堂上说外语时，我充满自信。						
19	我担心我的外语老师会随时纠正我犯的每一个错误。						
20	在外语课堂上当老师叫到我时我能感到心跳加速。						
21	外语考试我准备得越充分就觉得越糊涂。						
22	对在外语课前做好充分准备我不觉得有压力。						
23	我总认为别人的外语比我说得好。						
24	在别人面前说外语时我感到很难为情。						

题号	问题	1	2	3	4	5	说明
25	外语课堂节奏很快，我担心落后于别人。						
26	与上其它课相比，我觉得上外语课时更加紧张。						
27	在外语课堂上说外语时我感到紧张和困惑。						
28	在去上外语课堂的路上，我觉得非常有把握并且感到轻松。						
29	当我听不懂外语老师说的每一个单词时我就觉得紧张。						
30	学说外语要知道许多语言规则，我对此感到不知所措。						
31	我说外语时害怕别的学生笑话我。						
32	与讲该门外语的本国人在一起时我很可能觉得轻松自在。						
33	当老师问我没有事先准备好的问题时我就觉得紧张。						

III. 外语课堂焦虑问答题

1. 你为什么在外语课堂上感到紧张和担心？

2. 为了减轻你的外语课堂焦虑，你认为你自己可以做些什么？

3. 为了减轻你的外语课堂焦虑，你认为你的外语老师可以做些什么？

谢谢您的参与！

ABOUT THE AUTHOR

Jinyan Huang (Ph.D.) is an associate professor of TESOL and Assessment at the College of Education, Niagara University. Before coming to Niagara University, he was a linguist and desktop publisher at Lionbridge Technologies in Boston. He had also worked as a university English teacher in the People's Republic of China. He completed his Ph.D. (2007) in cognitive studies (Measurement and TESOL) at Queen's University in Canada. As part of his Ph.D. program, he studied at the Centre for Research in Applied Measurement and Evaluation at the University of Alberta in 2004. He earned his M.A. (2000) in TESOL and also a Graduate Certificate (1999) in TESOL from Brigham Young University.

Dr. Huang's areas of research centre on ESOL learning, assessment, leadership and policy issues. Specifically, he is interested in the following four issues: a) ESOL students' learning challenges and coping strategies; b) factors or level of factors that affect ESOL students' learning outcomes; c) ESOL assessment issues (reliability, validity, and fairness) in schools and universities; and d) the uses of data for supporting ESOL leadership and policies. In today's increasingly multicultural societies, these research interests have practical and policy implications. Such a focus enables Dr. Huang to concentrate on the use of his research expertise in ESOL cognition, generalizability (G-) theory, item response theory (IRT), structural equation modeling (SEM), and hierarchal linear modeling (HLM).

Dr. Huang's recent work has been published in *Assessing Writing*; *TESOL Journal*; *Language Assessment Quarterly; The Modern Languages Journal; Journal of Quantitative Analysis in Sports*; *International Journal of Business and Social Science*; *International Journal of Applied Educational Studies*; *The Canadian and International Education Journal; The Journal for the Practical Application of Constructivist Theory in Education*; *Journal of Instructional Psychology*; and *Education.*

INDEX

F

G

H

I

J

L

M

U

W